MADONNALAND

AMERICAN MUSIC SERIES

David Menconi, Editor

MADONNALAND

AND OTHER DETOURS INTO FAME AND FANDOM

ALINA SIMONE

UNIVERSITY OF TEXAS PRESS
AUSTIN

Requests for permission to reproduce material
from this work should be sent to:
Permissions
University of Texas Press
P.O. Box 7819
Austin, TX 78713-7819
http://utpress.utexas.edu/index.php/rp-form

The paper used in this book meets the minimum requirements of
ANSI/NISO Z39.48-1992 (R1997) (Permanence of Paper). ∞

Design by Lindsay Starr

Library of Congress Cataloging-in-Publication Data

Simone, Alina, 1974–, author.
Madonnaland : and other detours into fame and fandom /
Alina Simone.
pages   cm — (American music series)
ISBN 978-0-292-75946-6 (paperback : alkaline paper) —
ISBN 978-1-4773-0890-5 (library e-book) —
ISBN 978-1-4773-0891-2 (nonlibrary e-book)
1. Madonna, 1958– I. Title. II. Series: American music series
(Austin, Tex.)
ML420.M1387S46 2016
782.42166092—dc23
2015028441

doi:10.7560/759466

If you don't like me and still watch everything I do.
Bitch, you're a fan.

Madonna's Instagram,
April 13, 2015

CONTENTS

MADONNALAND

ONE

CONSPIRACY IN BAY CITY, OR, WHY IS MADONNA'S BIRTHPLACE THE LAST PLACE IN AMERICA WHERE SHE IS ACTIVELY CONTROVERSIAL?

The first thing you see as you enter Bay City, Michigan, heading down M-25 West, is a sign commemorating the 2008 state championship win of the All Saints High School's bowling, baseball, and softball teams. Farther down M-25, beyond a historic district lined with the nineteenth-century homes of lumber barons, a sign celebrates the sister cities of Ansbach, Germany (capital of Middle Franconia), and Goderich, Ontario (home to the world's largest undergound salt mine). Yet a third sign, located a few blocks north, announces Bay City as the hometown of Katie Lynn Laroche, Miss Michigan 2010. None of these signs are unusual for a quiet city of thirty-five thousand tucked between the Mitten State's thumb and forefinger, but their subject matter does tell you a few things: that Bay City isn't above a little self-congratulation, that you don't have to be Helen Keller or Martin Luther King to have your name immortalized in painted metal on either end of M-25, and that Bay City doesn't necessarily have a surplus of sign-worthy things to say about itself. Insofar as the third point goes, that turns out not to be true. The top-selling female artist in

history and one of the most famous women alive, Madonna Louise Veronica Ciccone, was born in Bay City on August 16, 1958.
A fact commemorated by the city exactly nowhere.

I'd been commissioned to write a book about Madonna, a
project I'd taken on with enthusiasm, even bluster. After all, I still
had my original copy of *Like a Virgin* on vinyl, an archive of back
issues of *Teen Beat* magazine, and a Slinky's worth of calcified
black rubber bracelets in my parents' closet back home. I'd spent
more than half my life surfing the sine waves of Madonna's career
and could rattle off frighteningly banal details about her sex life,
her workout regime, and her stance on the gifting of hydrangeas,
not to mention the unfortunate rodent problem she'd experienced
of late at her $32 million compound on East Eighty-First Street,
where a rat had been glimpsed scurrying into the bathroom while
she discussed the possibility of collaborating again with Britney
Spears during a video chat with the online radio show *Saturday
Night with Romeo*.

Looking back, these qualifications were perhaps less than PhD-
strength.

The logistics of writing a new book about Madonna, I soon
discovered, were crushing. Google Madonna's name and the
mother of Jesus is nowhere in sight. There is just a tide of accomplishments and accompanying pop-culture analysis waterfalling
endlessly through more than 34,100,000 websites, a nearly forty-
page Wikipedia entry, thousands of magazine and newspaper
articles, and a half-dozen biographies and documentary films to
eventually ciphon through a vast network of social media sites,
flooding your feeds and blocking your every social-media orifice
until you find yourself scrambling for the lifeline of an "unfollow"
or an "unlike" button lest you wake up one morning screaming with Madonna factoids oozing from the palms of your hands
like weeping stigmata.* Trying to ingest it all, let alone wreath it

---

* "The complete [Madonna] press file would probably yield enough recyclable pulp
to keep what's left of the Amazon rain forest from the saw for several months." This declaration was made in the introduction to *The Immaculate Collection*, back in 1990.

in words, feels like trying to give the population of Indonesia a hug—a task further complicated by the fact that both are simultaneously growing.

Getting people close to Madonna to talk to me was also no easy task. She is a powerful woman and most of her friends would prefer to remain that way. (One potential interviewee right away stated bluntly: "I am very expensive.") As for those who *were* willing to talk, the problem, I soon learned, was that they had been talking for a very, very long time, and their recollections had long since crystallized into sound bites that ricocheted dispiritingly through the web.

So I began my research in Bay City partly out of journalistic duty, partly out of desperation. Knowing one would basically need a DNA kit to link Madonna to her remaining kin in Bay City, I maintained hope of finding some tiny stone left unturned in the giant gravel pit of Madonna studies. Instead, I learned that I was just the latest in a long line of confused pilgrims to arrive here only to find no sign of Madonna. Not at her grandmother's former home on Smith Street, which attracts fans from as far away as Japan; not at the Calvary cemetery where Madonna famously treated her mother's grave like a yoga mat in her filmic tour diary *Truth or Dare*; nor at any of the other local landmarks carefully enumerated by sixty-nine-year-old retiree Edward Sierras when he went before the Bay City Commission to propose a Madonna museum and hometown bus tour back in 2008—a proposal that was politely shelved.

The local media haven't failed to notice the lack of Madonna signage, and have in fact made something of a beat out of its absence. In 2012, the *Bay City Times* published a story about an Argentine film crew who arrived to gather footage for a Madonna documentary but found so little to film that, in a kind of self-negating feedback loop, they ended up interviewing the very

Bay City Times journalist assigned to cover them. Another story describes the local melee on Madonna's fiftieth birthday, when reporters from both Ukraine's Inter TV and German public radio arrived in Bay City expecting a big celebration, but instead found two guys pounding out an acoustic cover of "Like a Virgin" in a local bar. The *Bay City Times* went so far as to dispatch a video crew to capture the German journalist's doomed effort to scrape together a story: his awkward phone chat with Madonna's ninety-six-year-old grandmother, Elsie, during which Madonna was seemingly never mentioned; his live interview with Madonna's fourth cousin, who may or may not have ever shared a sofa with Madonna. The *Times* also recorded the German's bewilderment over the fact that nothing had been done locally to commemorate the most famous female performer of all time. His interview with the *Bay City Times* eventually morphed into a mournful PSA addressed to the people of Bay City to please "make more about the fact that she was from here."

Cruising down Smith Street, it's easy to see what all the fuss isn't about. The former home of Madonna's grandmother, Elsie Fortin, has been converted into an eldercare center by its current owners, but aside from the addition of a wheelchair ramp, remains much the same; 1204 Smith Street gives off that woozy suburban ennui. I could practically feel the bored, endless tattoo of a basketball vibrating through the soles of my shoes. It is a single-story ranch house with a brown-shingled roof that sits on the corner of the most normal-looking street in America. I stare at it, trying to will Madonna to life. But of course, it wasn't Madonna who lived here, but "Nonni" Ciccone. And really she didn't live here all that much.

Bay City is where Madonna's grandmother grew up, where her mother, Madonna Louise, was born, and where her parents were married, yet Madonna's parents never made their family home in Bay City. At the time of Madonna's birth, her father, Silvio

Ciccone, and her mother (who was also named Madonna) were living in the Detroit exurb of Pontiac. Later they moved to the nearby city of Rochester, where Madonna attended high school.

Still, Madonna's family roots in Bay City ran deep. Madonna's grandfather, Willard Fortin, was a manager at one of Bay City's oldest businesses, H. Hirschfield Sons Co. Together, he and his wife, Elsie, raised eight children at their modest home on Smith Street. When Madonna's mother died of breast cancer at the age of thirty, she left six children behind—Madonna and her five siblings—Martin, Anthony, Paula, Christopher, and Melanie. Elsie Fortin stepped in to help them. Christopher Ciccone describes their grandmother as "a second mother" and the house on Smith Street as a "haven" from the strict household presided over by Silvio Ciccone and their stepmother, Joan (the former housekeeper, whom the children promptly cast in the role of Voldemort when she married their father). The Ciccone children, Madonna included, spent many summers and holidays in Bay City, and Madonna quietly helped support her grandmother up until her death in 2011. She returned numerous times over the years to visit, making stops at the old home on Smith Street and at St. Laurent Brothers, a candy shop that was one of her favorite childhood hangs. When Elsie Fortin died, at age ninety-nine, Madonna brought her four children to Bay City to attend the vigil service.

According to her family, Bay City also has sentimental significance for Madonna. Five years ago, Madonna's older brother Martin told the *Bay City Times*, "Bay City holds a real personal place in her heart, I know that for sure," going on to describe the summers they spent bridge-jumping into the Kawkawlin River and "smelt dipping" with their uncles. (For this image of a young Madonna in thigh-high waders, shining a flashlight into a shallow stream with a heart full of hope for fish, I would like to thank Martin Ciccone.) According to Martin, Bay City has found its way into many of Madonna's lyrics, and parts of the video for "Oh Father" were filmed in the local cemetery where their mother is buried. Shortly before her death, Elsie Fortin herself told the *Bay City Times* she believed Madonna had a special feeling for Bay City, but then added somewhat ominously, "I don't think she thought that Bay City liked her too well."

It's true that not every town or city with a famous native daughter throws up a congratulatory sign or plaque, but the fact that Bay City hadn't done so—and the ongoing, very public, process of community introspection on this topic—was something I'd begun to find more intriguing than the ordinary details of Madonna's childhood summers there. A feeling that only intensified when I found out about Stevie Wonder.

Wonder, who is eight years Madonna's senior, was born only fourteen miles away in the neighboring city of Saginaw. Not only is there a monument marking the place where his childhood home once stood, but in 2012 Saginaw launched Wonderfest,* an annual celebration in the singer's honor. Stevie Wonder left Saginaw for Detroit with his family when he was only four. Nonetheless, go to the City of Saginaw's website and it will tell you Stevie was born there. Go to Bay City's website, and it will tell you a national barbeque contest named the "Pig Gig" was born there. So why is Stevie (who has yet to attend a single Wonderfest) celebrated in Saginaw, while Bay City remains mute on Madonna? The answer, as any local conspiracy theorist will tell you, has its genesis in a controversy nearly thirty years old.

Bay City wasn't always doggedly indifferent to Madonna. Back in the summer of 1985, the mayor even offered her the key to the city.† At the time, Madonna was riding a swell of critical and popular acclaim for both her role in the film *Desperately Seeking*

---

* Saginaw's Wonderfest is not to be confused with Wonder Festival, the world's largest collectibles festival, held in Japan.

† It so happens that 1985 was also the year Saginaw awarded Stevie Wonder with a key to the city. Detroit had presented Wonder with a key one year earlier, and Wonder would also go on to earn a key from the city of Lansing, where he attended high school. (At this point the singer can basically unlock most of south-central Michigan.)

Susan and the decade-defining *Like a Virgin*. But this wasn't just a gesture of goodwill on behalf of then-mayor Timothy G. Sullivan (a Republican who didn't exactly fit the Madonna-fan demographic). Sullivan was canny enough to see the boon Madonna's business could bring to Bay City. He was openly quoted in the papers expressing his hopes for a Madonna "homecoming" show; Madonna's grandmother claimed that Sullivan contacted her at least seven times asking for help in persuading the singer to come to Bay City. But just days after his announcement, news leaked that nude photos Madonna had posed for during her early years in New York City were about to be published in *Playboy*. Suddenly, Sullivan had a change of heart.

"The key represents the citizens of the community," Sullivan told the *Bay City Times*, and "it would no longer be in good taste" to bestow such an honor on Madonna. The only other key Sullivan had presented during his short tenure had gone to a nun in her late eighties who was retiring from the local parish of St. Hyacinth. Sullivan made a big deal of the contrast between the two, which is weird because even before Madonna was featured in *Playboy* mysteriously petting a kitten shirtless, she had already built an entire career around being pretty much the opposite of a nun.

Whereas no one, perhaps not even Madonna herself, seemed to notice she had been offered the key to Bay City, the taking-back-of-the-key made national headlines. Sullivan managed to inject his frantic backpeddling with some measure of humor; the day after reneging on the key, he offered Madonna the city's second-highest honor. "A nice gold pin," he told the press, presuming she had "something to pin it onto."

To the surprise of no one, Madonna didn't drop by city hall to pick up her pin when she played the Pontiac Silverdome two years later. But a few days before that concert, she did refer to her birthplace for the first time on national television. In an interview with Jane Pauley for *The Today Show*, she called Bay City "a little smelly town."*

Her quip did not go over well.

Now there are those in Bay City who maintain there is a causal connection between these two events; the mayor's grandstanding precipitated the star's rudeness, generating enough local antipathy to power a grudge well into the next century. But it's doubtful that Madonna's comment was meant as any kind of tit-for-tat, especially given her very public (and rather unMadonna-like) apology later that week. "I do not think Bay City is a stinky city," she told the crowd of more than fifty-six thousand fans who showed up at her Silverdome concert in Pontiac. "I said it smells bad. I didn't say that about the people." Madonna explained that when she called her hometown smelly, she'd meant it literally, referring to the Dow petrochemical and cracking plants located downwind of her grandmother's home.

One problem with the apology was that, well, Madonna was not known for being sincere. The other problem was that her slip-up was the most famous reference to Bay City ever made on national television (one that remains enshrined on the city's Wikipedia page to this day). It left a simmering swathe of the local public feeling reactant and ill-used, like Madonna had dropped a stink bomb on Bay City from her Learjet, leaving them to clear the air with their tiny paper fans.

Strangely, Madonna's "smelly town" comment struck the opposite chord with the mayor who replaced Tim Sullivan; when I called up Mike Buda to discuss the scandal and its aftermath, his first words regarding Bay City's alleged odor were, "Madonna was absolutely right."

Nobody wanted to listen to her, Buda told me. Air pollution from the gas refinery and a neighboring beet sugar plant was in fact so bad that the EPA forced the industries involved to pay a

---

* She actually referred to Bay City as a "little smelly town in northern Michigan," although Bay City is in central Michigan.

cash settlement to families, like those of Madonna's grandmother Elsie Fortin, with homes in the Banks neighborhood. Whether it was a gesture in support of Madonna's budding role as environmental activist or simply an effort to dispel the bad juju generated by the Sullivan feud, Buda decided to re-offer Madonna the key, privately and quietly, shortly after he took office in 1991. Remarkably, the original key Sullivan had intended to give Madonna was still kicking around city hall. Eight inches long with a gold finish, the key had a clover-shaped head and Madonna's name engraved on the flattened stem. Alas, it wasn't to be; Madonna's publicist never responded to Buda's email.

It would be another seventeen years before Madonna would again be offered the key. Charles M. Brunner became the third mayor to offer Madonna the key to Bay City, and the second to have his offer make national headlines. But unlike either Sullivan or Buda, Brunner was a musician himself and a genuine fanboy. "I remember the first time that I saw you," Brunner rhapsodized in his letter to Madonna. "It was on a program that ran on Saturday evenings and you were singing 'Like a Virgin.'" He worked all the angles, telling Madonna how he used to be a drummer, that he and his wife had been married at Visitation Catholic Church, just like her parents, and they now lived around the corner from Elsie Fortin's place on Smith Street. Airbrushing over the bitter op-editorializing of the Sullivan regime, Brunner informed Madonna that Bay City had always been proud of her achievements and expressed his deep desire to mark her accomplishments with its highest honor.

Offering Madonna the key to the city was just one of the efforts to commemorate the star put forth by Bay City politicians that year. Not to be outdone, Guy Greve, president of the Bay Arts Council, announced he wanted to commission a sculpture of Madonna striking one of her iconic poses, while City Commissioner Chris Shannon (himself the frontman of a local band, the

Swaggering Rogues) pledged to create a Madonna tribute album. One would be forgiven for thinking Bay City Hall had turned into a gay disco, but this was 2008, and 2008 was Madonna's year. She was being inducted into the Rock and Roll Hall of Fame. She was turning fifty. She was tongue-kissing Justin Timberlake in her video for her top-ten Billboard hit "4 Minutes." She was shooting her *tenth* cover for *Vanity Fair*, cradling Earth in her hands. She'd become, quite simply, *a thing*—to dislike her now seemed almost churlish. And as the only hometown listed in her Hall of Fame bio, Bay City was receiving a groundswell of positive attention. For a moment, it actually seemed possible that Madonna might do for Bay City what Elvis did for Tupelo, Mississippi.

When Madonna's father, Silvio Ciccone, promised Brunner he would pass the mayor's letter along to Madonna, hopes were running high. The *New York Times* even ran an article with the headline, "Bay City to Madonna: Come Home." And then . . . ? Nothing. After a few months of silence from the Madonna end, all talk of homecoming concerts, crotch-grabbing statues, and tribute albums vanished like so many fanciful chalk drawings after a hard summer rain, and the *Bay City Times* resumed its mournful vigil over landmarks unnamed and tourist dollars lost.

Of course, the real question you might be asking isn't why Bay City lacks a Madonna sign, but why I can't seem to get unstuck from what most writers would consider, at best, a throw-away anecdote one might use to dress up a more impressive paragraph full of revelatory facts and insights that bring new heft to Madonna's biography. I tried to justify my inefficiency by telling myself that gaining an in-depth understanding of Bay City would help me better understand the impetus behind the rebellion that drove Madonna to leave Michigan and launch her epoch-defining career. Or that the Bay City signage controversy was just a reflection, writ small, of America's own divided views on Madonna.

But these are the lies I told myself to forestall the truth. And the truth was—I was failing.

What I needed was an inroad. A miraculously overlooked acupuncture point that would respond in some unique way to my touch alone. I'd been approached to write this book because I had once been a singer myself. Like Madonna, I was a girl who grew up lonely and alienated in the suburbs before winding up in New York, where I struggled for years, played bottom-rung clubs, and hustled for the same dignity-eroding "opportunities" advertised in the back of the *Village Voice*. It made sense to think I could use this slim cord of empathy and shared experience, if not to scale the Madonna Matterhorn, then to at least gain a foothold.

Only it didn't make sense because my career, such that it was, had mostly been defined by failure; my albums sold in the low four digits. More than that, I was, by nature, a lover of failure. A cherisher of the small and the daunted. A flame-holder for sad, ignominious efforts, doomed by the disinterest of the masses, but cherished by a handful of lonely men and women with coffee-stained teeth who still read books on paper. Quite simply, it was not possible for me to un-ironically put myself in the shoes of a superstar/sex symbol/cultural icon/billionaire entrepreneur named after the mother of Christ.

By contrast, I could relate to the people of Bay City. They had regular jobs and hobbies. They had *last names*. They picked up the phone when I called. And they were facing a tacit choice, which was whether or not they wanted Madonna to represent them. Whether they wanted to become, in effect, Madonnaland.

Bay City has known boom times. In the mid-nineteenth century it developed a thriving lumber industry, with an estimated fifty mills. A hundred years later, it had grown into a shipbuilding hub, providing warships and freighters to the US Navy during World War II. But with every boom came a bust, and Bay City emerged from the recent global financial crisis, and the collapse of the automobile manufacturing industry in nearby Saginaw, with a median income well below both the state and the national average. In a time of economic uncertainty, it made sense that some locals were beginning to take stock of their hometown's less conventional resources, and to wonder if Madonna might just be the thing to save them.

Gary Johnson was one of those people.

Gary has a different theory about the Madonna logjam. He believes Bay City, at its core, is a conservative place and that a silent but influential majority has worked the invisible levers of power to ensure nothing ever got done on the Madonna commemoration front. Whether this is true or not, the perceived anti-Madonna vibe has worked a weird kind of geomagnetic reversal in Bay City, forcing supporters of the superstar underground, like members of some kind of radical resistance movement, to set up their shrines in distant malls and car shops.

Gary Johnson, known locally as "Dr. J.," is the unofficial leader of the pro-Madonna faction, an oft-cited figure in the various *Bay City Times* articles on the signage issue. A former public school-teacher and lifelong resident of Bay City and nearby Essexville, Gary is also the founder of the Michigan Rock and Roll Legends Hall of Fame.* The MRRLHoF display on the wall of Bay City Motors, a vintage car dealership, includes a copy of *Like a Virgin* and an accompanying 8 x 10 glossy photo of Madonna; it is one of only two places where you will find any mention of the star in her birthplace.

It's hard to overstate the depth of Gary's passion on the Madonna-commemoration issue, a passion he has channeled

---

* In 2005, when Johnson first got the idea for the Hall, he sent a note thanking Terry Stuart, CEO of the Rock and Roll Hall of Fame in Cleveland, for the inspiration. Stuart promptly wrote back to say if he didn't change the name, Gary would be sued. To prove he was serious, Stuart told him he was already in the midst of suing another website, the Jewish Rock and Roll Hall of Fame, for trademark infringement. (Demonstrating an almost staggering lack of humor, Stuart pressed on with the suit even after the defendants offered to change the site's name to the Jewish Rock and Roll Challah of Fame. They were forced to settle, and the site is now called Jews Who Rock.) Thus the mouthsome acronym MRRLHoF was born.

to large degree into exhaustive historical research. His article "Madonna Misconstrued" on the Michigan Legends website is by far the most elaborate account of the Sullivan key flap and its aftermath. To wit: in 2008, after an unnamed official made a side comment to Gary about Madonna being undeserving of Mayor Brunner's offer of the key to Bay City, he went to city hall and unearthed the modest spiral notebook where the city's key recipients had for years been documented. In a blog post titled "Madonna—We Have Her Key," Johnson explodes the myth that the key to Bay City was an honor reserved exclusively for hospice workers, policemen wounded in the line of duty, and elderly nuns. "The St. Patrick's Day Queen gets a key each year, as does each year's Miss Bay County," Johnson wrote. "So did the Polish Dance Team in 1997. The winners of various boat races in town have also been so honored." Author Mickey Spillane got a key to Bay City when he visited in the 1990s, Gary went on, as did his sexy sidekick, the busty actress Lee Meredith, better known as "The Doll." This dismal accounting made even Madonna's passive contribution of increasing Bay City's number of Google hits worth contemplating.

Gary looks back at the key debacle of 1985 as a missed opportunity of epic proportions—Bay City's Waterloo. "I believe Madonna would have relished the chance to shine here, a place that held many of her childhood memories," he writes in "Madonna Misconstrued." "Instead, when Madonna was catching flak from all sides regarding the nude photos and probably feeling more than a little threatened, her hometown, through the actions of its mayor, turned its back on her."

As a symbolic gesture, Gary and his wife, Lynn, decided to make the four-hour drive to the Rock and Roll Hall of Fame in Cleveland in March of 2008 to watch Madonna's induction ceremony on a closed-circuit TV, so that "someone was there to represent Madonna's hometown." On his blog, he described the thrill of seeing "Bay City" flash up on the screen beneath Madonna's name and expressed the hope that his gesture on behalf of Bay City might "lead to other positive events."

When we first spoke in the summer of 2013, that hope had yet to be realized.

Gypsies Metaphysical Superstore is the only other place in town to promote the Madonna connection. Four years ago, Marianna Super, the owner of Gypsies (then called Mavericks), held a customer vote to decide whether she should name her new Brazilian blend "Smelly Lil Town Coffee." Despite other alluring options, like "Espresso Yourself," Smelly Town won. In addition to the coffee, Gypsies displays a four-by-five-foot photograph of Madonna framed in gold behind the espresso machine, and a ten-foot drawing of Madonna's astrological chart that takes up an entire wall. It is no mere decoration; Marianna, who was born at Mercy Hospital, just like Madonna, and who is also slender, blonde, and impossibly energetic, spoke like a seasoned sommelier on the topic of Madonna's cosmology.

"Madonna is a Leo and Leos love being on stage," Marianna told me. "She's Virgo-rising, which signals perfection, criticalness, precision, and she also has Saturn in the fourth home and mother, which means she never had a childhood, never had a mother. That's why she's independent and cares about other families." I asked Marianna whether Gypsies' Madonna displays had garnered any negative response. It's exactly the other way around, she insisted. "People say, 'Oh my Gosh, was Madonna born here?' and I say 'Yes, that's why she is perfect!'"

But according to Marianna this enthusiasm doesn't extend far beyond Gypsies' walls. She agrees with Gary's theory that a mysterious core of well-placed haters are responsible for the signage stonewall. "Why doesn't Bay City recognize her as a powerful, rich, grassroots person, and why don't they do anything about it? Because the older stuffy people have *all* to say in this town," Marianna told me, "and they don't want change."

But who were these Madonna minimizers, and what were their motives? Absent any hard evidence that such a conservative forcefield actually existed, I could only remain skeptical. Then Gary told me to talk to Ron Bloomfield, author of a 2012 book called *Legendary Locals of Bay City*. A book that *did not include Madonna*. Since this did seem like an odd, and undoubtedly deliberate, omission, I looked up Ron, who was also the Director of Operations and Chief Historian at the Bay County Historical Museum (another Madonna-free zone). Ron turned out to be eminently reasonable when I asked him why neither the museum nor his book mentioned Bay City's most famous export. Madonna did make the shortlist for his book, Ron explained, "but the shortlist turned out to be four pages long." Forced to toughen his criteria, the issue of Madonna's exclusion came down to the difference between "born" and "raised." In Ron's view, even though Madonna was born in Bay City, she was raised in the Detroit suburbs of Pontiac and Rochester Hills—cities that properly deserved the hometown crown. I got off the phone feeling vaguely chastened for implying Madonna's Bay City connection was greater than it was. *Legendary Locals of Bay City*, I imagined, was filled with stories of bonafide, born-and-bred, library-card-carrying, local Chamber of Commerce types who had helped grow their community from a humble cluster of log cabins on the east banks of the Saginaw River into a thriving city with nothing more than sweat and ingenuity. Just to make myself feel worse for insinuating Madonna belonged in this group, I clicked over to Arcadia Publishing's web page for *Legendary Locals*. In the descriptive blurb, I found only one example of a "legendary local" from the book: Annie Edson Taylor, who at age sixty-three became the first person to go over Niagara Falls in a barrel and survive.

A quick Google search yielded the following supplementary information: Taylor didn't actually move to Bay City until she was fifty-nine years old (by this definition of "raised," Madonna, who is only fifty-seven, has yet to *be* raised), and the few years Taylor spent in Bay City were mostly notable for her many attempts to move elsewhere (Sault Ste. Marie, San Antonio, Mexico City), which she finally succeeded in doing—a mere three years after she arrived. Worse, the sixty-three-year-old was only driven to toss her cork-encased body into a 188-foot hydro-canyon out of financial desperation; she couldn't make a living in Bay City and hoped the stunt would provide a windfall that would keep her out of the poorhouse.* "I might as well be dead as to remain in my present condition," she told a reporter en route to Niagara Falls.

I sensed the real reason Ron excluded Madonna from *Legendary Locals* wasn't about semantics, or even politically conservative qualms over her controversial oeuvre; he simply loved characters like Annie Edson: flawed, ordinary people whose stories would end up remaindered if it weren't for the careful stewardship of historians like him. Madonna didn't need his help, whereas Annie Edson Taylor did. But for Gary Johnson, there was something galling about the glossing-over of Madonna's roots in Bay City. He knew too much about the Ciccone family and their heartbreakingly normal house on Smith Street. About how "Nonni" loved the jolt in her stomach when her father zoomed over the Marquette Avenue viaduct driving into town, and the long summers she spent watching the mysterious freighters unload along the Saginaw River. And it bothered Gary that no one else knew these things too.

But whether damned or lauded by its mayors, ignored or exalted by its citizens, Madonna has nonetheless never been forgotten here; Bay City orbits Madonna like a lonely Teflon moon. And the future is theirs to write. Will her underground supporters prevail in their quest to commemorate her, or will the state

---

* It didn't—Taylor died in a poorhouse in Lockport after unsuccessfully trying to make a living off her Niagara acclaim.

of suspended animation continue as Bay Citians await a different sign—one of acknowledgment and reconciliation from Madonna herself?

Or will Bay City decide it would rather hold fast to its lost histories and faded heroines, becoming in the process something like the opposite of Madonnaland: the city that shunned fame?

TWO

SEEKING REFUGE FROM '80S ROCK, OR, WAS MADONNA ACTUALLY AN OUTSIDER ARTIST?

Failed books are generally buried like the sad, literary stillbirths that they are. Either that or they are reborn as PR fodder, providing the triumphant backstory to a bestseller. In my case, neither was true. The problem, I was realizing, wasn't just with the lakebed of existing information about Madonna, but with my own filter. I wanted to embrace Madonna in the fun, party-starting spirit that so much of her music embodies, but whenever I sat down to write about Madonna or read about Madonna or do any other Madonna-oriented things Madonna probably hopes that everyone on the planet wakes up to enjoy each morning, I was surprised to find a deep well of hostility.

I was a child of the '80s but came of age in the '90s, during the brief but incendiary era when raw, strange, and difficult music miraculously thrived, and maladroit people who never wanted to "find a groove" or "hit the clubs" could finally just sit in a dark room and feel bad to a great soundtrack. Given the lay of the musical land today, that era is clearly over. A war had been fought, and while the side wearing flannel landed a few solid blows, the ultimate victory lay with the sleek and shiny mainstream artists brandishing songs bought from Swedish hitmakers. Madonna was a general in that war, and Madonna won. Oh, some may say that Madonna herself—her music, her brand—is no longer culturally relevant in 2015, but what I mean to say is that unlike Kurt Cobain's punk-inflected, nihilist rock, Madonna's aggressively commercial, hypersexualized model of pop stardom remains dominant. She has spawned a lineage of taut, billion-dollar blondes—first Britney Spears, then Lady Gaga, and now Miley Cyrus. Though they tweaked the Madonna model in different ways, their success proves that herein lies a pop element as timeless as blue jeans and as infinitely plastic as vanilla ice cream. Whether we like it or not, we are all living in Madonnaland.

And once upon a time, I was happy there.

Like most girls who blinked into musical consciousness in the stonewashed '80s, my relationship to Madonna's music takes the shape of an inverse parabola. It began in bliss, somewhere around fifth grade, when V-66, a poor-man's version of MTV, began airing on local television in New England. I was an overweight, brooding, Russian American girl growing up in the Massachusetts suburbs during the Cold War. There was nothing remotely Madonnalike about me, and that's probably why I was so mesmerized by Madonna's unself-conscious happiness. It was an aspirational thing. I was a dumpy, dark-haired, and awkward kid, but wanted to be thin, blonde, and beautiful. And to dance on a giant cake. Plus her songs were meth-level addictive.

The image of the '80s that hogs the most space in the cultural imagination is largely an urban one, of mohawked-scenesters, coke-snorting Wall Street execs, and the all-night dance clubs where the two co-mingled. But out in the suburbs, life was breathtakingly drab. We dressed in khakis and loafers and white button-down shirts. Chain stores gobbled up independent shops like

Pac-Men gobbling pellets. Indian food was considered exotic. No one was gay. My town had no bars, no clubs, no theaters. Aside from two Chinese restaurants and a tiny movie theater that once showed *The Gods Must Be Crazy* for six consecutive months, there wasn't much fun to be had that didn't require a car, birth control, or psychotropic drugs. Madonna's bombastic oeuvre offered the perfect escape vehicle. She was the poster girl for a downtown hedonism that I could only hope awaited me at the far end of the rainbow. Which in my case meant a university seven miles away.

Then (like now) there was nothing uncool about loving off-the-shelf mall music. Out in the burbs, that *was* music. Sure, there were radio stations that played non-Billboard hits, but after a steady diet of over-caffeinated pop, glam metal, and melodramatic ballads, they came off as effete, too difficult to comprehend. Imagine growing up reading nothing but *People* magazine and suddenly being expected to appreciate Baudelaire's *Fleurs du Mal* in the original French. That's what trying to appreciate Minor Threat or the Butthole Surfers felt like in suburban Massachusetts in the mid-'80s after being raised on KISS 108FM.

Then all at once, everyone I knew came to see this whole situation as a generational tragedy. We'd been raised in a cultural airport—a shiny but sterile island of manufactured scarcity, where the few things for sale are all overpriced and stale. It came to feel more than a little sinister—the same ten songs on the radio in high-rotation, the jackhammer of mass marketing reaming your innocent earholes at every opportunity, the supersized rock stars with their supersized videos and supersized egos. A decade of hyperbole had opened a collective ache in our hearts for the kind of authenticity that couldn't be staged. And there, of course, was Madonna, at the top of the shrink-wrapped heap, putting the "M" in Monoculture.

I know most people cite Nirvana as the band that crushed the '80s pop juggernaut like some giant, hollow can of Fanta. But to me, Sinead O'Connor will always be the one who made the first dent—a salvo launched with no greater weapon than her honest wrath. In 1989, when *Nevermind* was still a year and a half away, Sinead got up on the huge Grammy stage alone wearing torn jeans and a black halter top and sang a strange, searing song called "Mandinka" from her debut album, *The Lion and the Cobra*.* The songs on this album, which Sinead wrote mostly herself while still a teenager, sounded like nothing else on the radio. This was complicated, powerful, and brutally intimate music. After one listen, I was transformed. No longer could I ever be satisfied with the karaoke-ball simplicity of Madonna's music, the way "star" always had to rhyme with "far" and "together" with "better." (Er, sort of.) They were both wonders of the world, but Madonna was a manmade work of brawn and patience—a Great Wall of China—whereas Sinead was a freak of nature, as wild and inexplicable as the Aurora Borealis. For the rest of high school, I used *The Lion and the Cobra* as a kind of Rorschach test. A positive association identified a person as a friend for life. A negative one was fine too—it just meant you had no soul.

For the better part of the decade, liberal-minded girls like me had been encouraged to adopt a convoluted form of postfeminist logic when contemplating the female icons of the era. By carefully folding your ideals into a tiny origami crane, you could arrive at the prescribed conclusion: that someone like Madonna, who was rarely the sole author of her songs (let's not quibble about this), could never get by on sheer musical talent alone (ditto), and never failed to present herself as anything but maximally sexy and fashion-fit, was some kind of role model. In Sinead, I saw an artist who not only wrote and produced her own songs, but possessed a voice of such glacial beauty that all comparisons fell away like a bunch of random, squiggly lines tacked next to

* OK, she lip-synched; it was still the '80s.

her name. And the kicker was this: with a face that could have been torn from the pages of an illuminated manuscript, here was a woman who went to heretical lengths to make herself *less*, not more, beautiful. Sinead could easily have gone the Madonna route (collagen implants, personal trainers, a lifetime of calling an Altoid after-dinner "dessert"); instead she wore band T-shirts and scuffed boots, and shaved her head. Every girl I'd ever met longed to be beautiful. *More beautiful.* Perhaps the bravest thing a beautiful girl can ever do, in the eyes of another girl, is to make herself ugly. (Paradoxically, in Sinead's case, making herself "ugly" only made her more beautiful. Really, nothing aside from a dioxin-and-road-salt facial could make Sinead ugly, but hey, at least she was trying.) The idea that being beautiful was a choice, an option that a pop star could reject in the hopes that more attention might actually be paid to her music, felt absolutely radical in the '80s.* As Sinead explained in an interview with *SPIN* magazine in 1992, "The women who are admired are the ones who have blond hair and big lips and wear red lipstick and wear short skirts, because that's an acceptable image of a woman. Because it's safe. It's not threatening. It's not intimidating. I'm threatening and I'm intimidating because I don't conform to any of those things and I just say what I think."

Sinead was the anti-Madonna, not just to me but to everyone—including Madonna.† In 1990, Sinead became the first woman to ever win an MTV Video of the Year award. *Nothing Compares to You*, which features Sinead stark and naked singing into the camera, beat out Madonna's high-budget, clinically

---

* Not that Sinead was perfect—crackpot conspiracy theories poured from that beautiful face with distressing constancy. But even Sinead's inchoate politics felt more genuine and urgent than any of Madonna's excommunicable offenses. When Sinead tore up a photo of Pope John Paul II on *Saturday Night Live* in 1992 while chanting the word "evil," there was nothing glamorous about it; she dealt her career a blow from which it never recovered. When Madonna wrapped her lips around a sexy black Jesus in the video for *Like a Prayer*, and danced among burning crosses, she looked beautiful doing it and earned millions from the controversy generated.

† Sinead claims that Madonna once told her she "looked like she'd had a run-in with a lawnmower" and was about "as sexy as a venetian blind."

choreographed, David-Fincher-directed video for *Vogue*. The *Philadelphia Inquirer* called it a "grit-over-glitz" victory, and it indeed felt like a watershed moment for American taste. Sinead won three awards that night, Madonna none. Sinead would go on to sweep the nominations for the 1990 Grammy awards just as Madonna entered her Dark Ages.

In another two years Madonna's coffee table book, *Sex*, her NSFW video for *Justify My Love* (which was banned by MTV), the contortions on display in her video tour diary *Truth or Dare*, and her record-breaking use of the word "fuck" on *David Letterman* (fourteen times) would achieve the hitherto unthinkable: making mankind collectively wish that a woman would please just put her vagina away. Her album *Erotica*, released that same year, would become her worst selling of the decade.

And we, the children of the '80s, took a vicious pleasure in laying her low.

At that time, there were things about Madonna I would not have wanted to know, facts that contradicted my comforting potted narrative of good vs. evil. I was not yet old enough to know that every person contains multitudes. And the things that might have changed my mind about Madonna were buried deep in the liner notes of her bio. Like that in high school, Madonna quit the cheerleading squad after discovering ballet, and transformed herself from a pretty, well-liked jock-dater to a moody artiste who confounded her peers. She threw away the laurels of high school popularity to flaunt her armpit hair and to star in avant-garde student films. In fact, throughout her late teens and early twenties, Madonna didn't give a toss about being conventionally pretty or conforming to anyone's standards. She earned straight A's, but committed herself to the insular pursuit of modern and classical dance. At age nineteen, she ditched a four-year scholarship at an impressive university to move to a city known as much for its murder rate as its art scene—alone. At that time, with her scissored hair, men's shirts, and torn jeans, Madonna really didn't look so different from Sinead. But this messy, arty, skateboard-riding Madonna was never *our* Madonna. Our Madonna arrived on TV screens and record store shelves a fait accompli, as cash-for-product, the ultimate insider. The enemy of the Real and the Authentic.

The truth is that Madonna started out as a freak and a loser, not so different from the flannelled freaks and losers I hailed as saviors. She was a college dropout who slept on stained futons for years in depressing, fourth-floor walk-ups, fronting a series of go-nowhere bands. There were years of rejection, poverty, and false starts. And when she did finally land her first record deal, her handlers had dim hopes for her chances at stardom. The industry execs tasked with promoting her debut didn't view Madonna's suppurating sexuality as a marketing godsend, but rather, as some icky barrier to overcome. The best marketing strategy her label could come up with was to pass her off as black (which explains why her photo was excluded from copies of her first single, "Everybody"). As Reggie Lucas, producer of her eponymous debut, explained, "Managers, record company executives, we met a lot of those people together, and the first thing that you would see is these people were just appalled with Madonna."

"I mean, they just thought she was just some *horrible* person," Lucas told me. "They used offensive language to describe her, and without naming names, some of these people became her lifelong business employees and representatives. But as soon as it became clear that she was going to be a major economic suc-cess, they very quickly reversed their decision."

By the time Lucas met Madonna, he had already won a Grammy for co-writing a hit for Stephanie Mills. He'd also served as a sideman for jazz icon Miles Davis, musical polyglot Sun Ra, and Grammy-award-winning vocalist Roberta Flack. Given this pedigree, I didn't exactly expect Lucas to effuse about Madonna's

native talent, or her outsider status. But it was these exact qualities that Lucas insists first drew him to Madonna.*

"Well, the first thing a lot of people would say was 'oh, she
can't really sing.' But being someone who's a fan of all sorts of
DIY music, I liked the sound of her voice," Lucas said. She wasn't,
as her critics alleged, patched together in the studio from a zillion
different takes. Madonna really could sing, he told me. She could
improvise on the tags. She was *good*.

"I heard something very vivacious and energetic and crisp
about what she was trying to do, and it was supported by so
much personal energy. I like things that are musically exciting to
me. Is the message delivered and is it delivered in a sincere and
satisfying way? [Madonna] had a heartfelt feeling about who she
was and what it was about. She didn't pre-think it and do the
demographic research. Not only do I think it was not calculated,
I don't think it was something she really concerned herself with.
I mean if there was a direction of message with Madonna, the
message went one way—it went OUT. She just put it out there
and no feedback was taking place. To be honest," he shrugged,
"my approach didn't differ that much from the jazz musicians I
had worked with."

Sincere, heartfelt, and uncalculating—these are not words
usually associated with Madonna. And I could almost feel my
brain being jello-molded into an unfamiliar new shape as I con-
templated them. Madonna's pop-music flirtation with, as Lucas
put it, "the edge of sexual mores," was also something new. If
you look at the smattering of top female artists of 1982—the
year Madonna's debut EP, *Everybody*, was released—you'll find
the sweet-faced soft-rocker Olivia Newton John, the leather-
clad hard-rocker Joan Jett, and the comparatively melodic and

* Lucas also had plenty of reason to disparage Madonna. His role in launching her
career was minimized by Madonna and her then-boyfriend Jellybean Benitez (who
remixed her first album) after *Madonna* began scorching serious pop-chart terroir. Thanks
to recent journalist efforts by Chris Williams, writing for the *Atlantic*, and Sean Howe,
writing for *Rolling Stone*, as well as Wikipedia-monitoring vigilance on the part of Lucas's
children, this is starting to change.

cerebral Chrissie Hynde. Madonna wasn't soft, hard, or cerebral. Rather, her music was a marriage of disco, an almost pathologically reviled genre at the time, and New Wave. One wouldn't think that Madonna muddling this strange musical cocktail with her own dose of sex appeal would be so attention grabbing (after all, sexiness was quickly becoming de rigueur on the video dial); but Madonna's sexiness was different, more brutal. And it would only become more so as time went on. Instead of vaguely gesturing at something sexy potentially happening behind heavy curtains on the nineteenth floor of a hotel across the street, Madonna was more intent on conjuring thoughts of real blood-engorged organs meeting and greeting. She truly, deeply *loved* sex—and whether you could see her or not, you still felt it. Even over the radio, Madonna was a world-class eye fucker.*

* Walking down Third Avenue in Manhattan one morning, I spotted a black-and-white poster about the size of a handbill wedged between two doorways. "COST FUCKED MADONNA," it read, in bold, iconic letters. A few doorways down, there it was again, nested in a monochromatic tangle of similar declarations featuring "Cost." Dutifully, I took a picture.

Once home, I Googled the cryptic declaration and discovered that "Cost" was the nom-de-plume of graffiti artist Adam Cole, and that he'd begun wheat-pasting his *Cost Fucked Madonna* mantra all over Manhattan more than twenty years ago. Back in the early nineties, Cost Fucked Madonna became an underground catch-phrase, spurring a healthy trade in knock-off T-shirts ("ELVIS FUCKED MARILYN") and other merch. Cole himself was well on his way to cult status when he was arrested in 1995 for defacing a Queens *Tribune* box with a sticker. The Queens Criminal Court sentenced him to two hundred days of community service, three years probation, $2,180 in fines, and mandated psychological counseling. Far more depressing for Cole, he was also publicly unmasked—as a twenty-six-year-old cab driver from Rego Park, Queens.

Now, after seventeen years of silence, Adam Cole is back. *Cost Fucked Madonna* posters began reappearing on the streets of New York in 2012. That same year, Cole was interviewed by *Vandalog*, a graffiti-art webzine. And though his art now sells for up to $30,000, his answer to the perennial question—Did you really fuck Madonna?—remains unchanged: "You don't kiss and tell."

I decided to pose the question to Madonna herself during her recent "Ask Me Anything" live e-chat on Reddit. After all, Cole was a friend of subway scratchiti artist RP3, one of Madonna's early boyfriends, and he also claimed to have worked at Limelight and Palladium—both popular '80s dance clubs and known Madonna haunts. Unfortunately, mine was not among the more than eight thousand questions Madonna chose to answer that night. But it does seems pretty unlikely Madonna fucked Cost; my back-of-the-napkin math seems to show he would have been around twelve when Madonna was in her club-going heyday.

But all the evidence supports Madonna's sincerity in this aspect of her work as well; her art is highly sexualized because *she* is highly sexualized. In terms of both breadth and depth, Madonna has always been a woman of unusual appetites—a unicorn—living according to the laws of the sexual utopia promoted in her videos, where no lover is rejected on the base of race, gender, age, or sexual orientation. As a teenager, she was already scoring triple-hitters by seducing Christopher Flynn—the openly gay, black ballet teacher twenty-eight years her senior. But when she reached New York, her sexploits reached the status of legend. Lovers provided crash pads, jobs, guitar lessons, rehearsal space, instruments, lunch, hope. These included her first musical collaborators (Dan Gilroy, Stephen Bray), the DJ who brought her to the attention of Sire Records (Mark Kamins), and the producer who fanned her fame to greater heights ("Jellybean" Benitez). Those who didn't make the cut, like her first manager, Camille Barbone (who was a lesbian), or filmmaker Stephen Lewicki (who got no further than licking blueberry yogurt out of Madonna's ear in Battery Park one day), have publicly expressed regret on that score. Erika Belle, Madonna's best friend at the time, tells stories about Alphabet City cruising expeditions with Madonna, where she would window-shop hot Latino guys as casually as someone doing a bodega run for dental floss. And according to Barbone, by the time her first demos landed on Seymour Stein's desk, when she was twenty-four, Madonna could claim more than a hundred lovers. Madonna was the feminine equivalent to a ladies' man: a gentlemen's lady. Of course, there's a reason this term doesn't exist. Women aren't allowed to enjoy and practice sex-as-sport the way men do. Compare Madonna to famously libidinous artists like Jim Morrison or Mick Jagger, and the sexual double standard becomes clear.

The feminist criticism (and my own subconscious one, when I compared Madonna to Sinead) was that she insulted women by playing into male stereotypes, conforming to the image of the perfect sex toy—skinny, blonde, and scantily clad—and reveling in her own objectification. The implication here was also that Madonna had adopted this carnal persona in a calculated bid to gain a competitive advantage at the dawn of the music video age, when visual shock tactics did as much to fuel sales as killer hooks. She addressed criticism of "setting women back 30 years" in a 1984 interview with MTV, the year *Like a Virgin* was released. "I don't think that I'm using sex to sell myself, I think that I'm a very sexual person and that comes through in my performing, and if that's what gets people to buy my records, then that's fine. But I don't think of it consciously, 'Well I'm going to be sexy to get people interested in me.' It's the way I am, the way I've always been."

In other words, Madonna was being nothing if not authentic when she stripped down, danced lasciviously, and sang lyrics like, "Some girls, they like candy, and others, they like to grind, I'll settle for the back of your hand somewhere on my behind." Sex to Madonna was what flowers were to O'Keefe, what Tahiti was to Gauguin. What else was she supposed to sing about?

The other thing that made Madonna's assent improbable, Lucas explained, was that even though her music was aimed at the mainstream, it wasn't commercial in ways then deemed "cool." Her celebration of disco carried more than a whiff of defiance at a time when white-bread rock was ascendant. The rock industry's intentional de-coolification of disco was actually a convenient smokescreen for both racism and homophobia, Lucas said. "In the early '80s," he told me, "it was about bands that were not integrated, that didn't play anything that sounded like disco music or even blues. It had a very demographic, cultural price of admission. All that stuff—burning disco records—I mean come on, it was also very anti-homosexual. It was about 'we don't like all these gay guys' and 'we don't like all these drag queens' and 'we don't like all these black people who play this disco music.' It's not 'cool.' And so it became a convenient way to speak out against those people." By contrast, the dance scene to which Madonna belonged was a crossover scene in the best sense of the word, both inclusive and integrated. Madonna became the vanguard of that scene, and an enthusiastic promoter of gay culture. Something that even earned her the grudging approval of Kurt Cobain back in 1993. "In a way I respect Madonna . . . because she introduced some subversive things and it has nothing to do with sex," he told MTV. "I'm talking about the introduction to the vogue dance which originated in the gay clubs in the mid- and early '80s. She was always supportive of things like that which I think is really cool."

Cobain was right—Madonna's celebration of gay culture, especially at a time of epic AIDS paranoia—*was* cool. There were a lot of cool things about Madonna, not least of which that she was an aggressively self-made woman. Perhaps my real problem was the multitudes Madonna contained. Philanthropist, businesswoman, provocateur, actor, director, children's book author, seducer of stunning young men . . . And yet I was still struggling to find the one Madonna I really wanted to write about it.

Then, for a moment, it seemed as though I'd found her. While poring over interviews with those who'd been close to Madonna in her pre-fame days, I began coming across eyewitness accounts of her spellbinding, near-shamanistic performances on the dance floor. Eye-widening descriptions along the lines of, "I had not truly lived until I saw Madonna dance and will now move across the country/dump my fiancé/change my sexual orientation just to be with her." I recognized in these descriptions my own reaction upon first hearing Sinead O'Connor sing. Even people who vigorously disliked Madonna went mushy on the subject of her dancing. When I spoke to Scott Severin, a nodding acquaintance of Madonna's back in her Danceteria club-going days, his recollection of her was strikingly harsh. "There is no way to overstate her ruthless ambition to be a star," Severin told me by phone. "She wasn't interested in small talk, the New Wave scene, the punk scene, men, sex, other bands—she was interested in furthering her dance and music career. She was interested in being a huge, huge star. She had more than enough charm, gumption, manipulative abilities, and maaaybe just enough talent."

But when I asked whether he remembered how Madonna danced, his tone immediately shifted. He was there the day she filmed the dance scenes for *Desperately Seeking Susan* at Danceteria. "You know what it looked like?" he said. "She wasn't dancing demonstrably; she wasn't dancing to necessarily be exhibitionist, but she was dancing extremely gracefully and blissfully." Madonna was *always*, Severin admitted, a lovely sight on the dance floor.

It is no surprise that Madonna was first attracted to ballet, that most Teutonic of disciplines, but when she entered the world of dance at fifteen she was already behind. By the time Madonna walked into Christopher Flynn's second-floor dance school, many of her peers were already on pointe. Instead of letting this daunt her, Madonna simply resolved to work twice as hard. Her determination, as well as some kind of ineluctable fire in the way she moved, won Flynn over; she quickly became his protégée. Madonna recalls the moment Flynn first noticed her the way most people recall first falling in love.

"He was my first taste of what I thought was an artistic person," she told *Time* magazine in 1985. "I remember once I had a towel wrapped around my head like a turban. He came over to me and he said, 'You know, you're really beautiful.' I said, 'What?'

Nobody had ever said that to me before. He said, 'You have an ancient-looking face. A face like an ancient Roman statue.' I was flabbergasted. . . . I'd never had a sense of myself being beautiful until he told me. The way he said it, it was an internal thing, much deeper than superficial beauty."

It's easy to see what drew Madonna to Flynn; as an openly gay black man and former-naval-officer-turned-dancer, Flynn would have stood out in New York City circa 1974—in Rochester, Michigan, he was flying the freak flag high. It was Flynn who inspired Madonna to be brave, to dream big, to act decisively as the sole arbiter of her destiny.

He soon began taking Madonna along with him to art galleries, playing the cultural Henry Higgins to Madonna's Eliza Doolittle, feeding her books and classical music. A couple of years later, when Flynn was recruited to join the dance faculty at the University of Michigan, Madonna followed him (probably the last time she would follow anyone anywhere) with a full dance scholarship. By this time she'd made up her mind to become a Serious Modern Dancer. Nine months later, when Flynn told her, "Stop wasting your time in the sticks. Get your little butt to New York City," she gave up her free ride to college.

That summer, Madonna was one of a half-dozen students selected out of three hundred to win a scholarship for a six-week workshop hosted by the American Dance Festival in Durham, North Carolina. She beat out those three hundred dancers again to capture the lead in Richard Mascal's July 1978 write-up of the American Dance Festival's debut in Durham for the *Charlotte Observer*:

> Her name is Madonna Ciccone, and her face matches her name. Round eyes, arched eyebrows, finely drawn mouth—Da Vinci would have loved it. It is a theatrical face, a dancer's face. And she has a dancer's body—thin as a blade, lithe and agile. Doll-like, she looks as if she'd snap in a strong wind.

She wouldn't. Dancers are strong. A sophomore at the University of Michigan in Ann Arbor, Madonna has gotten stronger this summer. Halfway through a vigorous six weeks at the American Dance Festival at Duke University, she works early and late.

"It's pretty draining and demanding," Madonna says, munching Granola Crunch mixed in Dannon lemon yogurt. "You spend all your time dancing, every day, day in and day out."

In many ways, Madonna is what the American Dance Festival is about.

Everything Madonna would later become known for is already on display here, in what is probably her first press mention: her physical allure, her strength, her work ethic, her unnerving self-assurance, and her supernatural ability to become the focus of attention regardless of the milieu. Even as a yogurt-eating scholarship kid at a summer dance workshop, Madonna already invited metaphor, already *stood* for something.* By the time that workshop was over, she had secured a coveted place in Pearl Lang's prestigious dance company in New York.

Of course within months of arriving in New York, taking the pulse of the club scene, and picking up her first guitar at the urging of boyfriend (and future bandmate) Dan Gilmore, Madonna ditched the avant garde for stardom. The rest, as they say, is history. Or, simply—present.

But here's the mystery: where did it go? Whenever I watched videos of Madonna dancing, either live in concert or in her music videos, her moves just seemed kind of . . . aerobics-y. A lot of air-punches. A lot of step-class type arm reaches. Skipping, clapping, jumping-jack extensions. It definitely doesn't smack you in the face the way, say, Prince's crotch-defying air splits or Janet Jackson's frictionless shimmy does. There's no singular style on display in these early videos, not even a subtle stamp of originality, like

* In a 2015 interview with *Raleigh News and Observer* music critic David Menconi, Mascal also mentioned that Madonna was "one of the most self-absorbed persons I had ever met."

the electrifying wrist flick with which Michael Jackson famously adjusted his fedora in *Smooth Criminal*. Madonna's modern dance bonafides were *legit*, yet it was a well-documented fact that she would rather spend precious video seconds sucking on her finger or raking her fingers through the kudzu of her hairsprayed bangs, than, you know, dancing.

I became obsessed with tracking down footage of a young Madonna dancing—really dancing—unchoreographed, uninhibited, and unaware of the camera's eye. At a party, at Danceteria, in Detroit somewhere, jonesing for a glimpse of the dance supernova who engulfed early collaborators like Stephen Bray, Dan Gilroy, and Mark Kamins, and who convinced Pearl Lang, one of the grande dames of modern dance (a Martha Graham protégée for God's sake!) to take her on as a student. I perform the digital equivalent of a deep cleanse colonic on Google in search of such a video, but in the end come up dry. Then, while rewatching *Lucky Star* for what must be the 118th time, I develop an insidious new theory—*Madonna is holding back on us*. The theory went like this: after Madonna determined the world of modern dance was a cultural backwater, she intentionally dialed down Lang's downtown influence as well her native dance abilities in order to maximize her popular appeal. After all, half the fun of loving Madonna in 1983 was matching the dance routine in *Holiday* step for step. And nailing it. The uncomplicated allure of her step-clap type dance style may have polarized critics, but it was an undeniable hit with the rest of planet Earth.

To test my theory, I contacted her younger brother Christopher, who responded to my email with a speed I normally associate with family emergencies. I explained that I was working on an un-explainable book about Madonna, and asked whether his sister might have been deliberately falling short of her abilities as a dancer. Before informing me that he charges $3,000 dollars for a forty-five-minute interview, and after ascertaining I was indeed serious, Christopher rejected my question as irrelevant. I had failed to understand, he told me; Madonna was all about the complete package.

Of course, Christopher—who wrote a cattily entertaining book about life with his sister and the dissolution of their relationship, which boiled down to a dispute over an interior decorating bill for exactly $45,000—knows best that *nothing* is irrelevant when it comes to Madonna. If anything, a question about her skill as a dancer should fall on the more relevant side of the ledger. "Complete package" irked me. It was the stock defense of Madonna-philes, as knee-jerk in its way as critics saying she can't dance, or can't sing, or that she's just a boob-slinging opportunist. Now that I thought about it, the entire pop-culture-consuming public could probably be divided into Complete Packagers and Incomplete Packagers on the topic of Madonna. But I wanted to take the package apart. I wanted to be left breathless, like Madonna's early boyfriend Norris Burroughs, after seeing her impressive spin-into-grand-jete move on the dance floor of Irving Plaza one night. Or to watch Madonna make herself "the vortex of the room," as she did one night at a disco near Detroit, a scene her college room-mate Whit Hill describes so breathlessly in her memoir *Not about Madonna* that for a moment it seemed Madonna's dancing had turned her gay.

I wanted Madonna's dancing to turn *me* gay.

But I also noticed that one group in particular had maintained a mysterious silence on the question of Madonna's dancing over the years, the group perhaps most qualified to offer an informed opinion: dance critics. On the rare occasion an expert did offer an opinion, it remained marooned in trade publications or schol-arly books. Sure, you'll find an academic analysis of Madonna's "floor-bound, indirect, twining body movements" in the anthol-ogy *Before, Between, and Beyond: Three Decades of Dance Writing*, but these observations weren't exactly accessible to the layperson. So I decided to take my inquiry straight to the top; I invited *New York Times* dance critic Claudia La Rocca over to watch some Madonna videos with me, to see whether she could decode Madonna's dancing for me. To show me what I was missing and make me a believer.

Over the course of an hour, we watched a number of Madonna's early music videos and concert footage, including a grainy clip of Madonna performing a piece by Elizabeth Bergman, one of her professors back at the University of Michigan. For the majority of this time, Claudia wore a squinty, vexed expression on her face. She peppered her comments with qualifications. "I think she's capable, she has training in her body." And, "You can see it in smaller moments, just with how she'll shift her weight or how a hip will open." But eventually she clicked stop and exhaled.

"I don't look at her dancing and go, 'This is really compelling and she's doing interesting things and look at all these influences and traditions she playing with,' in the way that I do with certain other people," she told me. Claudia did not think Madonna was holding back on us. She looked at me and shrugged.

"I guess I don't feel strongly one way or the other."

Of course it was ludicrous to begin with, this idea that I could learn to love Madonna through, if not force of will, sheer force of research. There was so much to admire, I kept telling myself. Her uncanny, hit-minting ability. Her fashion derring-do. Her successful, globe-spanning business ventures. Her ass. Some of her movies. Her lifelong, heartfelt support of gay rights and safe sex. Her more recent anti-ageism campaign, fought spiritedly in a bustier and leather panties. Her discipline. Her foundation, Raising Malawi, which builds schools, provides scholarships, and supports health care initiatives in a beleaguered Sub-Saharan country. Her ability to do a split at age fifty-five, photographic evidence of which she recently posted to Instagram. And yet, the more I dug into Madonna's past, the more interviews I read, the more I watched and listened and grappled with her Gigantosaurus-sized ambition, the further I drifted from any kind of central narrative. And now here I was, beached on some remote, uninhabited island with my conspiracy theories unraveled, nattering aloud to a lone palm tree.

This should have been when I gave up on Madonna herself and moved on to the thing that really interested me: fame. Both the strange and often tragic corollaries that accompany its overabundance, and the equally unnerving symptoms marking its absence.

That's not what happened.

THREE

MAGICAL CONTAGION, OR, WHAT HAPPENS TO MADONNA'S LONELY MOUNTAIN OF STUFF AFTER SHE DIES?

In 1994, in an interview with *Details* magazine, Madonna was asked what she planned to do with a barely-lived-in house she owned in Los Angeles. "I don't know," she quipped. "Maybe I'll open up Madonnaland." When I read this, I couldn't help but wonder whether there would ever be a Madonnaland, if not during Madonna's lifetime, then in the unthinkable event that she ever, you know, *passes*. I mean, what is going to happen to Madonna's lonely mountain of stuff when she dies?

As it turns out, there are a lot of people interested in Madonna's mountain of lonely stuff and at least one investment fund—Marquee Capital—whose valuation is almost entirely based on it. When I spoke to Chetan Trivedi, the company's founder, he went to great pains to assure me that *no* thought, none, zero, had been given to Madonna's death. That said, he absolutely believed that just like the Elvis museum, there would be a Madonna museum one day. And when that day came, Marquee would contribute. In fact, they've already begun launching exhibitions of their own Madonna collection, the most recent of which took place in

Macau (where Madonna's name is pronounced Mak Don Na) at the aptly named City of Dreams casino.

Looking at sales of Michael Jackson collectibles pre- and post-death, which sold for a gross profit of 250 to 800 percent, one could easily predict a similar trajectory for Madonna memorabilia. Trivedi is convinced that over the next five to ten years Madonna will break all kinds of auction records. This is why he declined what he described as an "interesting offer" made in Macau for the original costume Madonna wore in her 1985 moniker-making *Material Girl* video. The costume is likely worth more than $150,000 by now, Trivedi told me, but in some unspecified, possibly Madonna-less future, might rake in as much as half a million dollars.

Then again, maybe Madonna *wasn't* joking about opening Madonnaland; the most interesting thing Trivedi revealed during our correspondence was that authentic, high-end Madonna collectibles from the past two decades have become exceedingly rare for the simple reason that post-1993, Madonna began hoarding them herself, allegedly stockpiling costumes and other personal effects in a storage bunker somewhere in Los Angeles. It comes as no surprise given both the canny business sense Madonna has demonstrated throughout her career and the white-knuckled grip she's maintained over use of her music, likeness, and other creative assets that even the fate of her sweaty bustiers would not be left to the whims of the free market.

Social scientists have an explanation for why we put so much value into the private possessions of celebrities like Madonna: it's known as the magical law of contagion and refers to the belief that when people come in contact with objects, some part of their soul or essence rubs off on them. According to research conducted by Yale School of Management psychologist George Newman, we value the possessions that a "good" celebrity (as opposed to, say, Hitler) has actually touched (like clothing) more than other things they owned that they probably rarely came into physical contact with (like chandeliers). Such is our belief in the magical fairy dust of celebrity that we value Madonna's sweaty bustier even more if it *hasn't been dry-cleaned* since she wore it. Newman's research reveals we want these artifacts to remain pristinely unsanitized so as to better preserve their juju.*

I found the notion of magical contagion deeply compelling. It explained the feeling I got from talking to those who knew Madonna ten, twenty, even forty years ago, that they'd been somehow infected. Most of these people weren't living in the shadow of Madonna per se—they had led active and often interesting lives—but their contact with Madonna had lent them a strange sort of radioactivity. Whether they meant for it to happen or not, the significance of the time they spent with Madonna kept metastasizing, spurred by everyone else's outsized interest, until it became the official byline to their lives. It hovered over them, the very possibility of her, the remote chance she might suddenly remember them, swoop in to save or elevate them.

This notion of contagion might also apply to the entirety of Bay City, where Madonna once lived, played, and dipped for smelt. The contagion had spread to the people there, at least those who would like to see Bay City, in some small way, become Madonnaland. And people like Gary Johnson had in turn infected me. My instinctive attraction to underdogs (Bay City Madonna supporters) had quixotically overshadowed my instinctive dislike of overdogs

* Newman's research on magical contagion also reveals real differences between the kinds of people who value celebrity memorabilia and those who don't—differences that suggest there are larger forces at play when it comes to putting a premium on Madonna. For one thing, those who place more value on items owned by celebrities were less likely to come from places like India. Research subjects in eastern countries valued celebrity-owned rarities less than their western counterparts, even though they valued *natural* rarities (like dinosaur bones or moon rocks) about the same. Lovers of celebrity memorabilia were also more susceptible to other forms of magical contagion. They were more likely to refuse to eat soup that has been stirred by a "used, but washed, flyswatter" and were more likely to have had a sentimental attachment to things like teddy bears or blankets in their youth.

(Madonna herself), and now I too found myself cheering Gary on in his quest. As a storyteller, it wasn't hard to get caught up in the dream of cinematic closure; for Madonna to finally come home and accept the key to Bay City; for the anti- and pro-Madonna factions to end their bitter feud, join hands, and sing a good old-fashioned song about sex together; for the beginning of a Bay City renaissance with a Madonna cottage industry at its heart. Mostly I wanted these things because I really liked Gary, who reminded me of my favorite junior high social studies teacher crossed with Smokey the Bear, as well as the gentlemanly Ed Sierras, who had retained the domain names madonnabaycity.com and madonnabaycity.org since 2008, and whose emails to me always ended with news of the Michigan weather and the sign-off "Fondest Regards."

But without a concrete way to support Gary's commemorization cause, all I could do was sit in my New York apartment adding my own smattering of useless information to Gary's informal history of Bay City's troubled relationship with Madonna. Here the snow still lay deep and undisturbed over fields of factoids only marginally relevant to Madonna, and my heart quickened whenever I found one. Like the news that back in 1985, just after Timothy Sullivan refused to give Madonna the key to Bay City, the owner of a local tool-and-die shop took things into his own hands. *Literally*. Jerry Charboneau forged his own key to Bay City for Madonna.

"Me and the guys all kind of chipped in and spent some time and made a big brass key and engraved in it something like, 'To Madonna, the key to Bay City, the people who care.'"

At least, that's what Charboneau *thinks* the key said; he couldn't quite recall the exact inscription when the *Bay City Times* got around to interviewing him in 2008. He does recall that he brought the key to Madonna's grandmother, Elsie, who promised to deliver it to Madonna at her upcoming wedding to

Sean Penn. Charboneau's was a supersized version of the puny official Bay City key: eighteen inches long and custom mounted in a plush, velvet-lined case. When she returned from the wedding, Elsie told Charboneau that Madonna had been grateful for the gift.

Excitedly, I fired off a note with my findings. But it turned out I'd have to work much harder to surprise Gary, who already knew all about Charboneau and his key. My persistent enthusiasm for his cause, however, had an unexpected side effect; suddenly Gary was interested in raising the issue of the Madonna sign again. I told him that if he organized some kind of public event that might serve as a community forum on the Madonna issue, I could try pitching the lack-of-signage story to a national news outlet. A few days later he informed me that Ron Bloomfield, the same author who had excluded Madonna from his book, *Legendary Locals of Bay City*, had magnanimously agreed to let Gary make a presentation on Madonna's local roots for the Bay County Historical Museum's "Second Saturdays" program.

According to vague local gossip, the museum was the death-star of Madonna opposition. Ron admitted to me by phone that he would personally be perfectly willing to exhibit a high-quality Madonna artifact at the museum but feared that such a display might trigger a membership boycott. Obviously Gary would need all the help he could get, so I set about trying to unite the balkanized pro-Madonna camp in Bay City. When I wrote to Marianna Super, she immediately offered to host free Madonna horoscope readings at Gypsies Metaphysical Superstore on the day of Gary's event. Ed Sierras was even more enthused. "I feel like an old warhorse," he replied, "rejuvenated and ready for many more charges at the ignorance and ineptitude that abounds in BC."

Another person who might have been rejuvenated by the prospect of some good old-fashioned Madonna-frisson was her one-time local nemesis, former mayor Timothy Sullivan. Sadly,

Sullivan was unrejuvenable—he had died, suddenly, at the age of fifty-eight that September. Gary was particularly upset because now he wouldn't have a chance to interview Sullivan for his presentation. In all likelihood, though, Sullivan's take on Madonna hadn't changed. The *Bay City Times* had revisited the key scandal in an interview with Sullivan in 2008. The years had softened him up a bit—he conceded that Madonna's induction into the Rock and Roll Hall of Fame was "well deserved," and even that her long ago "smelly town" comment had some merit. But when asked directly if he'd like to see Madonna finally get the key to Bay City, he hedged like it was 1985: "I would welcome her back to Bay City," he told the *Bay City Times*. "We'd recognize her. I don't know. I probably would want to talk to her," he offered, before adding with what sounds like a note of pathos, "I was comfortable with giving a key to the city to a nun."

One thing my research turned up that I decided not to share with Gary was that Madonna had spent the first five years of her career lying about where she was born. Unlike Jesus, Madonna clearly didn't see her humble genesis as a plus. Nor were Pontiac or Rochester, the cities where she attended school, interesting enough to call home. It was a preoccupation her college roommate Whit Hill notes in her memoir, *Not about Madonna*: "I wish I was from Detroit," Hill quotes Madonna as confiding during one of their earliest conversations. "I live in Rochester. It's a suburb. I'm from a freakin' suburb."

Moving to New York after dropping out of college only exacerbated this perceived shortcoming. And within one year of arriving, Madonna *was* from Detroit—at least on paper.

"*I was born and raised in Detroit, Michigan, where I began my career in petulance and precociousness.*" This is how Madonna begins her charm-assault on director Stephen Lewicki, in response to an ad he'd placed in the pages of *Backstage* magazine looking for a "strong dominant woman" to star in his no-budget erotic thriller, *A Certain Sacrifice*. Whereas Rochester was located in one of the wealthiest counties in the US (and *the* wealthiest county in Michigan), Detroit had entered the nation's consciousness as a kind of urban apocalypse; in 1979, the same year Madonna sent her letter to Lewicki, the mayor of Detroit awarded Saddam Hussein the key to the city in gratitude for his cash donation to a bankrupt church. Even before she started singing, Madonna was already branding herself as a fallen angel emerging Mad-Max style from the embers of a dying city, all torn-mesh halter tops and dirty lace.*

Madonna went on claiming to have been born in Detroit for years—even after her debut album hit the Billboard top 10. In 1984, some five years after Madonna left Michigan, a mulleted MTV interviewer opened his interview with her with a casual, "So, you were born in Detroit . . ."

Spiritually and aesthetically speaking, of course, Madonna was born in New York City. Or at least reborn, in the sense that the transformation begun in Christopher Flynn's ballet studio when she was fifteen years old reached its natural point of chrysalis in New York, less than ten years later. New York is where Madonna formed her first band, starred in her first movie, and recorded her first album. It's the city that made her a star, and which she transformed into her playground. New York, in many ways, became Madonna's chief export—its fuck-you attitude, its poverty-chic fashions, its glittering ambition.

And the iconic Madonna-of-the-Lower-East-Side is probably how she will be best remembered. Living in New York now, I can easily imagine the stations of her cross: the former synagogue in Queens where Madonna's boyfriend Dan Gilroy first taught her how to play guitar (still inhabited by Dan Gilroy); the American

---

* It also goes to show just how much Madonna had learned about marketing herself in the short time she'd spent in New York: she ends the same letter with another small, but notable, untruth: she lists her birthday as August 16, 1959—one year late—banking on the notion that a sexed-up teenager will outshine her haggard twenty-year-old doppelganger any day. Correctly—she beat out more than three hundred competitors and got the part.

Music Building in midtown, the infamous music rehearsal com-
plex where she squatted for a year with collaborator Steve Bray
(still there, still sketchy); her former fifth-floor walk-up at 232
East Fourth Street (where a two-bedroom apartment now sells for
upward of half a million dollars); the former home of Danceteria at 30 West Twenty-First Street, where Madonna put her first
demos into the hands of DJ Mark Kamins (now a luxury loft building featuring "twelve full-floor, sprawling, private keylock lofts,
resplendent in air and light, with 50-foot-wide living rooms");
The Vault, the notorious S&M club in the meatpacking district
where Madonna shot parts of her *Sex* book (now Dos Caminos,
"Serving authentic and upscale Mexican cuisine, including fresh
guac and killer margaritas"); right up to the trio of linked town-
houses she currently inhabits on the upper east side, with a stable
of gladiatorial young men on hand to fetch her cucumber water.

Manhattan is Madonnaland. But the very qualities that make it
so ensure that New York doesn't *need* a Madonnaland. The same
can't really be said for out-of-the-way places like Bay City, where
major petroleum companies hide their cracking plants. These are
the kinds of places one tends to find celebrity-themed museums,
amusement parks, restaurants, and festivals—a phenomenon that
can feel less like an homage than a last-ditch economic development strategy. One that is just as likely to backfire.

Broadly speaking, there's a name for this sort of thing: Destination Branding. But when I spoke with Bill Baker, author of
Destination Branding for Small Cities, he was skeptical of mold-
ing the identity of a place to a specific celebrity, or as he put it,
the "George Washington Slept Here" model.* Celebrity status is
an unstable element, Baker warned. Even the biggest and most

---

* Coincidentally, I actually grew up a mile away from the Monroe Tavern, where
George Washington actually slept. Lexington, Massachusetts, known as the birthplace
of American liberty, is a destination more well branded than a veteran Yakuza. In fact,
my first job as a teenager was waitressing at a colonial-themed diner called "The Pewter
Pot," where I served Patriot Fries and Franklin Burgers, and had to dress as an eighteenth-
century milkmaid. In theory, the American Revolution was the kind of noble and lofty
"brand" everyone could get behind. In practice, this translated into gift shops selling
maple candy molded into the shape of dead Minuteman soldiers' heads and Boy Scouts

successful celebrity destination of all time, Graceland, is in for tough times when the cult of Elvis wanes.

According to some sources, that is already happening. Last year the *Wall Street Journal* ran an article with some troubling statistics: the number of visitors at Graceland in 2010 had dropped to 519,000 per year from 540,000 the year before, and bookings for Elvis impersonators in Las Vegas (where the Elvis-O-Rama museum had ominously closed) had fallen by more than 20 percent between 2011 and 2012. Of course, there are many who scoff at the idea that Elvis isn't forever. But even if The King's post-mortem appeal turns out to be finite, one could hardly call Graceland (which generated $32 million in revenue in 2012) a failed effort in destination branding. And though Madonna may not quite be Elvis Presley, according to Daniel Wade, the editor of the Paul Wade Collectibles (another top-tier purveyor of Madonna memorabilia) news service, she is still up there in the pantheon of stardom. "Can Madonna be ranked among names such as Marilyn Monroe?" Wade wrote. "I would say she is step below in terms of enduring fame, but that's not to say she isn't a terrific investment. To achieve long-term growth you must have a growing number of buyers entering the sector over the years and decades to come. Only the most iconic names can achieve this, of which I feel Madonna is one."

So there was some evidence that Gary Johnson's and Marianna Super's and Ed Sierras's dreams for Bay City could be realized. Ultimately, it would all come down to the fans. But I wondered: would Bay City, with its laid-back vibe and aura of genteel decay, be able to provide the right kind of environment for the legions who equated Madonna with wealth, bombast, and sky-high

waving signs reading "Voldemort was a Redcoat" at the battle reenactment on Patriots' Day. Was it Madonnaland? Of course not. But nor did Lexington conform to the ideals of its tourist brochures. Ask the kids about the best local spot to get high and they'll direct you to the Old Belfry Tower.

One thing you can say about Lexington's brand is that it endures. The Revolutionary War never goes out of style, and the shops lining Massachusetts Avenue can rely on a steady stream of tour buses hogging street-side parking from April to October.

production values? Would they really make the trip to Bay City? I mean, Madonna fans aren't necessarily cuddly, or easy to herd (by anyone who isn't Madonna). They don't, for example, have a cute name. Of the sixty-eight different fan monikers listed on Radio.com's "List of Music Fandom"—Taylor "Swifties," Phish "Phans," Justin "Beliebers," Britney "Spearleaders"—Madonna fans were noticeably absent.* As far as I could tell, her supporters were either part of the "Golden Triangle," an uber-VIP stage-grazing section reserved for diehard concert attendees, or members of "ICON," the official Madonna fan club. There was no global network of VogueHeads meeting in living rooms, S&M parlors, or Hard Candy Energy Bars—there was only the mothership, the oculus, the corporate funnel into which all Material Girl longing must inevitably channel itself: Madonna.com.

Could Bay City's efforts to honor her be doomed from the outset by Madonna's own monopoly over her fans' love? And who *are* these people, anyway? The fans so diehard that they would drive all the way to Bay City, Michigan, merely to see Madonna's name on a sign, or take a selfie with a modest plaque in front of her grandmother's old house?

I decided to find out.

Since Madonna has sold more concert tickets and more albums than almost anyone else, it stands to reason that she has fans—millions and millions of them. But I didn't know any. And no one I knew knew any either. Apparently there was some kind of invisible line separating those who loved Madonna from those who did not. And I wondered whether there was some accompanying set of character traits or preferences—a passion for disco or melodrama or calisthenic-style dancing?—that kept Madonna fans siloed from the people I knew, who liked dark rooms, coffee, and state-subsidized European films filled with existential despair. Then one day, quite by accident, I stumbled upon the

---

* It would, in fact, be interesting to see if there is some weird algorithm at work here. As Radio.com points out, the singer Adele has sold more than 10 million albums in the short span of her career, yet her fan base has not felt the need to self-name.

man who could answer these questions for me at a shop just around the corner from my apartment.

At forty-five, an age when most of us are starting to regret the blurry ankhs and Chinese proverbs inked on our still-dewy flesh during our college years, Joel Herrera* decided to get his first tattoo: a row of Madonna's initials inscribed on his inner arm. Within two years, his entire back was covered in hyper-vivid Madonna portraits culled from her album covers. When we met, he had just embarked on the Madonnification of his torso.

Knowing nothing about Joel beyond the fact of his tattoos, I went into our interview with some dark assumptions. The thing is, I didn't even know what these assumptions were, or that they existed, until they were quietly shattered—like when Joel told me that he had been a social worker for the past twenty-four years. What did I expect? That just because Madonna was a high-maintenance narcissist, all her fans must have jobs styling poodles or branding coconut water? Nor did Joel meet my idea of how a Madonna superfan should look. I was expecting a fit gay man, hair dense with product. A man with a high-rise apartment full of leather and chrome furniture. But Joel had black, shoulder length hair, and was consumptively lean. He had two heavy silver hoops dangling from each eyebrow that gave him a punkishly hangdog look. If we were playing "This Man is a Superfan of _____," based on appearances alone, I would have guessed Joy Division or XX. Oh, and he lives in a house in New Jersey.

But mostly, Joel and I didn't talk about Joel; we talked about Madonna. And how much he loved her.

It happened while he was a freshman at Trenton State College and his dorm-mate Tracy played Madonna's debut album for him. "As I listened to it more and more, I literally fell in love," Joel told me. Next came the videos, which were "killer," followed by the interviews, which revealed that he and Madonna had a lot more in common than a shared love of dance music: both were Italian,

---

* Not his real name.

both were Catholic, both grew up feeling alienated in the burbs. He attended his first Madonna concert in 1987, her "Who's That Girl?" tour, and has attended every tour ever since. Though the portrait on the cover of Madonna's debut album may not be his favorite Madonna image, it had the most symbolic value, which is why Joel elected to tattoo it on his back first, followed by the cover for *True Blue*, and then the portraits adorning the singles for *Justify My Love* and *Vogue*. (For his next tattoo, he's considering an image from *Express Yourself*.)

Since then, his interest, and concomitant investment in Madonna—emotional, financial, physical—has ramped up significantly. When Madonna's last album came out, Joel spent $5,000 on travel, tickets, and merch, and that's not counting the $3,000 he's spent on tattoos within the last two years. Nowadays when Madonna tours, Joel generally goes to every show in the tri-state area (usually nine or ten shows),* and he always gets the most expensive tickets, which cost around $350 at preferential, Golden-Triangle rates. When someone gets judgy about the amount of money he spends on Madonna, he likes to ask them where they went on vacation last year.

"Instead of a tan that will inevitably fade," Joel gains a much richer experience for his money. Ditto with the tattoos, which turn out to only be the latest incarnation of the Madonna shrine that takes up a room in his modest New Jersey home.

Some things in Joel's shrine:

· Practically every Madonna T-shirt ever made
· Madonna bumper stickers, books, buttons, tour programs
· Bespoke jackets Joel has had custom-tailored with photos from Madonna T-shirts (too frayed to wear) sewn into the backs
· Jewelry, bracelets, necklaces, and Madonna perfume (Yes, for women. Yes, he wears it.)

* Joel also informs me he is always careful to use the word "show" and not "concert" when describing a Madonna performance, and to refer to her as an "artist" rather than a "singer."

· Madonna dolls created by a woman who specializes in extreme modification of Barbies, purchased on eBay

Maintaining this elite level of fandom requires not only lots of money but also oceans of time and patience. Joel tells me about the time he and his friend Nick "literally locked themselves in the house" from 5 p.m. to 3 a.m., spending ten hours calling into a radio station in order to win tickets to a fan-only pajama party celebrating the release of *Bedtime Stories*. And about waking up brutally early so he could be one of the first fifty people at Macy's to buy items from Madonna's new "Material Girl" line, a prerequisite for gaining special access to another show.

The tattoos, of course, make a public fact of Joel's obsession. And while they have netted him some free concert tickets (through Madonna.com-sponsored fan devotion contests), they also provoke a lot of long looks at the beach. At least the response from his family and friends has been positive, Joel told me, except in the case of one relative. Their exchange:

Relative: You know that's permanent. What happens if you
   stop liking Madonna?
Joel: You do know me, right?

I had to admit, as a journalist, I found the monotony of Joel's love for Madonna exhausting. A graphic representation of his feelings for Madonna over time contained no peaks and valleys; it was simply a diagonal line going up and up and up. I asked him how he felt about Nirvana and the grunge era. Blank stare. His thoughts on Madonna's weakest-selling record? "*Erotica* was a great album." Other Madonna fans? "The *best* group of people. Accepting, friendly, social. Plus, they are just as addicted as you are!" Beyond the conversation-stopping aspect of his devotion lay the philosophical chasm dividing us when it came to the merits of Madonna's oeuvre.

"I can *hear* everybody else's music, but I *feel* Madonna's music," Joel told me. "You can't help but hear a song and relate it to your life," he added, before launching into an explanation of how *Ray of Light* helped him get over a bad breakup. I sat there wondering what Madonna's music had ever gotten me through. A bout of vacuuming? An all-night drive through the featureless plains of Nebraska? Joel's comments lay in stark contrast to my personal view that Madonna's best music was eerily feelingless, except in the case of her ballads, which struck you with a giant fist of feelings that only $5-million-per-song production can buy. It somehow agitated me that Joel didn't deduct any cosmic honor points for the profit motive that inspired these songs. Sad healing songs are supposed to come from sad, broken people, I wanted to say, who spend weeks or months gang-pressing their inchoate emotions through an actual instrument to arrive at something soul-stirring. Sad, healing songs aren't supposed to spring from a corporate whiteboard at Warner Music headquarters before getting farmed out to nameless ballad-writing professionals. It went against my sense of fairness. It was cheating! Snide little jerk that I am, I tried to prod Joel into recognizing that Madonna was not the sole auteur of her work. When he praised her series of children's books, I thought—aha!—and eagerly explained I had recently interviewed her ghostwriter, the woman who had, you know, written all the words in those books with Madonna's name on the cover. I was armed with other damning evidence—bitter denunciations by famous Madonna collaborators who had been minimized in the credits to their own songs; copyright infringement lawsuits from photographers claiming their models first struck those famous poses; song lyrics ripped wholesale from Gap ads (a settlement was paid). But Joel's mild surprise at the ghostwriting revelation was quickly replaced by benign acceptance. "Oh," he shrugged.

Oh.

Carl Wilson brilliantly skewered the indie crowd's manipulative play of the authenticity card in *Let's Talk about Love*, his book about coming to terms with the allure of Celine Dion. Authenticity, he argues, is just a convenient excuse to judge people, a morally acceptable way to declare your superiority over the Walmart-shopping, mouth-breathing hordes. Pitching myself into the gorge of Joel's fathomless love for Madonna had no doubt triggered the kind of "bewilderment and status vertigo" Wilson recently described in a blog post for NPR, "that makes you aware of your own smallness, your vulnerability and, yes, thus your shame. It undercuts any fantasy that your own lifestyle, traits and priorities might be universal—it tells you that you're specifically bounded by your own context, while other realms may be indifferent to your existence."

Wilson is right; I am a judgy, indie music revanchist who loves nothing more than a good glockenschpiel jam and a hot cup of single-origin coffee. I am bounded by my own context. I wish knowing these things could change my worldview or extinguish the quiet rage I felt when Madonna recently covered my favorite song by my favorite indie singer, "Between the Bars," by Elliott Smith, as part of her #secretprojectrevolution #publicitystuntthingee.* I wish I could just drink the wisdom of Wilson's words like an antidote to the disease of Painfully Niche Preferences; it would make writing a book about Madonna a lot easier.

It was nearing dinnertime, and the meat smells at the restaurant where we were drinking our wine were growing more insistent. But before Joel got up to leave, I blurted out one last question that I hadn't jotted in my notebook—one that wasn't even about Madonna.

"Are you a happy person?" I asked.

"I would definitely describe myself as a happy person," Joel nodded emphatically. "And part of it is being a Madonna fan.

---

* A rage similar to that which spurred Carl Wilson, also a huge Elliott Smith fan, to write his book after seeing Celine Dion defeat Smith to win the 1998 Oscar for Best Original Song.

Sometimes when I'm feeling kind of down, all it takes is one song and my mood changes on a dime."

It wasn't so much the answer that I found surprising, as the jolt of jealousy that shot through me. Throughout our hour-long conversation, Joel was wholly un-ironic when it came to his obsession with Madonna. This, in turn, had only stoked my feeling of superiority. After all, the life of a superfan, with its all-night radio giveaway vigils and income-obliterating merch consumption, is the kind of subject ripe for a Christopher Guest mockumentary. By contrast, I looked like a well-adjusted person whose interests remained happily constrained by the limited amount of time/energy/money at my disposal. But who was actually the well-adjusted one here? Joel *was* happy. And when I thought about my Madonna-hating friends, I couldn't think of a single one who would ever chirp, "I would definitely describe myself as a happy person" as decisively as Joel had. What's more, there probably wasn't anything of a non-alcoholic, non-narcotic, non-hallucinogenic nature that could turn our mood around the way "La Isla Bonita" could for Joel. There is a real happiness borne of the crowd, of immersing yourself in an echo chamber where your tastes are affirmed and amplified millions of times over, of surfing a million outstretched hands at the Atlanta Pavillion in Lisbon as Madonna croons "Bedtime Stories" above your head. Here in my apartment listening to the stark, individualist cries of suicidal punk singers, surrounded by the dead stock of forgotten '70s labels and hand-numbered vinyl releases that stand out like dead poky trees in an ocean of mainstream pop, I even feel some satisfaction in denying myself this pleasure.

But I wouldn't call it happiness.

FOUR

MADONNA MISCONSTRUED, OR, GETTING THE HELL INTO MICHIGAN

The same week I flew to Bay City for Gary Johnson's presentation about Madonna at the Bay County Historical Museum, I made arrangements to return my book advance. I decided I wasn't going to tell Gary; I thought it would be unfair to distract him with my literary psychodrama while he was preparing for his big day. In addition to garnering a big feature in the *Bay City Times*, Gary had also been interviewed on the local TV 5 and TV 12 news shows. When I talked to Ron Bloomfield, he told me the museum was expecting a capacity crowd.

But a few days before I flew out, Gary sent me an unexpected message. Subject line: Diehard.

Hi Alina,

I'm afraid I'm going to have to disappoint you and reveal that I'm not a diehard Madonna fan. I'm sorry if I gave you that impression. My reasons for writing and presenting things on her was based mainly on my disgust with the stupidity of Bay City's leadership for the past 29 years regarding the town's only rock and

roll star and the general narrow-mindedness that seems to prevail around here. The fact that she is a Michigan artist is what is
most important to me. If Madonna would not have been born
in Bay City and grew up in the state, I probably wouldn't have
done any of this.

Don't get me wrong, I like Madonna's music, especially the
'80s material, I greatly respect the stands she has taken regarding AIDS research and gay rights, and I think she is in a class by
herself in the field of music video. But as far as being a diehard
fan, it's the Beatles and the Rolling Stones for me!

Gary

I grabbed the opportunity to confess that I was no diehard fan
either. That I was, in fact, dropping the book but still flying out to
Bay City to support him.

Two days later, high above a patchwork of midwestern farm-
land, I stared out the window of the plane and felt bad about the
contract I'd signed, bad about the time I'd wasted, and bad about
being a quitter. But it was also the first time in months that I'd felt
truly free.

It was the coldest month of the coldest Michigan winter in at least
130 years. An hour after leaving the Flint airport I steered my rental
car down M-25, past the varying signage that made no mention
of Madonna, and over the frozen Saginaw River, which was stud-
ded with the colorful tents of ice fishermen. It was as though Bay
City had been stage-set for my arrival. The place couldn't have
seemed any more cold, remote, or out of time; I half expected
Hans Christian Andersen to come skating out from under the
bridge wearing hand-knit long johns. Even though the presentation didn't start until 1 p.m., there were already a few people
waiting by the door of the Bay County Historical Museum when
I arrived an hour early. Ron Bloomfield, goateed, sweatered, and

anxiously patrolling the lobby, took pity on me (it was seventeen degrees out) and let me inside. Gary, looking spry in a black suit with a tart, pink-collared shirt, greeted me with barely suppressed glee. He intended to drop a "bombshell" at today's presentation, he announced, before disappearing into the conference room to check on the projector.

Despite all the time I'd spent obsessing over Bay City's recent history, I realized that I knew next to nothing about its distant past, so I decided to use my spare hour taking in the museum's exhibits. In a darkened wing off the lobby, I perused photographs of the Native Americans that the early Saginaw settlers had displaced, walls of antique lumberjack tools, and exhibits on shipbuilding. Wall text described the local travails of the unfortunately surnamed Jacob Graverot, founder of the American Fur Company and one of the area's first white settlers, and the foreign travails of the 339th Infantry, a unit of Michigan men stationed in northern Russia during World War I. Then, somewhere amidst the industrial carpeting and money-saving lights and sort of depressing realization that the experience of visiting a history museum is not unlike reading a set of outdated encyclopedias while standing in a dim corner, I stumbled on a section of the museum that, although it did not mention Madonna, was strikingly Madonna-like in nature. It focused on the part of Bay City once known as Hell's Half Mile, a cluster of "saloons, variety theaters, gambling houses, resorts, brothels, and flop-houses" where hard-living lumbermen parted with their money, their pants, and not infrequently, their lives.

I spent a long time reading about Hell's Half Mile, especially the infamous Bay City "Catacombs," which author J. W. Fitzmaurice described in the book *The Shanty Boy* as a three-story den of vice where one could find "every facility for drunkenness, debauchery, and gambling . . . associated with deeds or robbery or even murder. Here in the darkness made visible by the flare and glare of the dirty lamps, day and night alike, were found congregated the lowest and most degraded of both sexes. Here the most horrible and obscene orgies were carried on with perfect impunity." And the Red Light Saloon, frequent scene of "fights, stabbings, low dances and vile wickedness." I learned the varied and colorful euphemisms for brothels ("pretty waiter-girl saloons") and hookers ("soiled doves," "women of too easy virtue"), and the sad fact that it was not uncommon for Bay City prostitutes to die after overdosing on oil of wintergreen, which was used to induce abortion.

Aside from a pale lager named after Hell's Half Mile brewed at the local Tri-City Brewery, no traces of Bay City's debauched past remained. The waterfront had been thoroughly sanitized, mostly by antique shops where the dealers definitely know the going eBay rate for a vintage saw bit. As it happened, St. Laurent Brothers, Madonna's favorite candy shop back when she still ate candy, was located on the former site of the Catacombs; I'm sure Madonna would have been thrilled to know what kinds of salacious deeds used to go down on the very spot where she was sucking her Red Hots.

By the time I emerged from the history-womb, the hall was packed and Gary's talk was sold out. I discovered him in the lobby, chatting with two blonde women who turned out to be former students. Both were wearing oversized T-shirts with Madonna's face blown up to a disconcerting size. As I approached I noticed that Gary was holding a black-and-white photo of a man wearing a long coat with one hollow sleeve tucked into a pocket.

"Willard Fortin lost his arm in a hunting accident!" Gary said excitedly. Willard Fortin was Madonna's maternal grandfather. I enjoyed the feeling of not having to pull out a notebook to jot down that he had one arm.

Gary gestured to a petite older woman nearby holding more photos, and introduced her as one of Madonna's cousins. We stood in the hall for a while, admiring antique wedding photo-graphs of Madonna's kin, pictures that she had probably never laid eyes on, before making our way toward the conference room. There a bizarre scene greeted us: row upon row of Bay Citians, many of them elderly, sitting quietly as Madonna writhed around in lingerie and clutched at her breasts on the oversized screen above their heads. For a half-hour, even though the music was loud enough that the bass tickled your spleen, no one moved or tapped a toe or said a word. It was impossible to gauge why these people had come, and whether they loved or hated Madonna. They seemed too silent to be either Madonna fans or Madonna haters. On the other hand, what else was there to do on a Feb-ruary Sunday in Bay City during one of the coldest winters on record? Then the music died, the lights dimmed, and Gary took the podium. He looked out over the field of raised heads.

"I have great affection for Bay City," Gary began.

Since the crowd was already quiet, it didn't have to grow quiet at his words.

"I have great affection for Bay City," Gary said again, which seemed a little weird because everyone had most certainly heard him the first time. Personally, I was a little surprised that Gary was going out of his way to reiterate his affection given the con-tinued frustration he'd voiced about the city and its conservative, slow-moving leaders, but then he added, "These aren't my words, they're Madonna's."

As it turned out, *this* was Gary's bombshell. He had done the one bit of research that no one else in Bay City had bothered to do in all the decades of antipathy over Madonna's smelly town comment; he'd gone and listened to the entirety of Madonna's interview with Jane Pauley that fateful day in 1987. And what he found was that the local paper (staffed, it would seem, with anti-Madonna, pro-Sullivan cronies) had cherry-picked Madon-na's words so as to maximize Bay Citians' indignation. In those pre-Internet days, once an interview aired, it was gone. If you missed it, all you had to go on were clips in the paper and snippets on TV. In this case, divorced from all context, those snippets came off as particularly damning. And no one questioned the *Bay City Times* version of the conversation, which omitted Pauley's follow-up question.

"So do you say 'little smelly town' with some affection or complete distaste?"

And Madonna's response:

"No, no, no! I have great affection for Bay City."

And if you go to YouTube and watch the footage (as I did once I returned home) you will see that Madonna says this laughingly, lovingly, *nicely*.

"What if I told you that Madonna didn't really put down Bay City during that interview," Gary continued, prosecution-style, "and that she was the victim of a newspaper article that took her words out of context? And that she has been stuck with a bum rap here in Bay City for over twenty-six years?"

The crowd was murmuring now, as though someone had emptied a small ziplock bag of mosquitoes into the room. There was more. Madonna's family had all come to her defense in the days following the local uproar over her comments to Pauley. In an interview with the *Bay City Times*, the Fortin family explained that when Madonna called Bay City a "smelly little town," she had actually been riffing on a family joke. Apparently Madonna's father, Tony, had a long-standing mock competition with her grandmother, Elsie, over whose hometown smelled worse—Bay City, with its petrochemical and cracking plant, or Tony's birthplace of Aliquippa, Pennsylvania, with its industrial steel mills. It was starting to look like the supernova-sized chip Bay City had been carrying on its shoulder for more than twenty-five years was all just the result of a giant misunderstanding.

But this wasn't even the best part of what was definitely turn-ing out to be a plane-fare-worthy event. The standout section of Gary's presentation wasn't the smelly town bombshell, or any other revelation about Madonna, but his meticulously researched exploration of the central deity in the Madonna Mythology, born, raised, and beyond a doubt *of* Bay City in the deepest sense: Madonna's mother, Madonna Louise Fortin.

Though she was only five when her mother died, Madonna has spoken at length about her mother's influence and how her early death shaped her character, creating that infamous thirst for attention and approval a planet's worth of adoration has yet to fulfill. "I probably wouldn't be in the entertainment business if I had a mother," she told MTV in 1998. "It was a very big thing in my life. It changed me. It turned me into the warrior that I am."

Yet Madonna's mother has always been defined more by her absence than anything else. What little we do know puts her at the far end of the personality spectrum from her flamboyant daugh-ter. By all published accounts, she was a woman of extreme piety, devoted primarily to two things: family and Jesus. Throughout her career, Madonna has highlighted the extreme contrast between herself and her mother in interviews with the press. "[My mother] would kneel on uncooked rice and pray during Lent," Madonna told *Spin* magazine in 1996. "I mean, she would sleep on wire hangers. She was passionately religious. Swooning with it. If my aunt came over to the house, and had jeans that zipped up the front, my mother covered all the statues. Turned the holy pictures to the wall."

The Freudian incongruity between Madonna and her chaste mother could launch a thousand dissertations, but were the two really polar opposites? The ying to the other's yang? As with all things Madonna, Gary believed there was more to Madonna Lou-ise Fortin than met the eye. It turned out that he had attended St.

Joseph's, the same high school as Madonna's mother, and had some old yearbooks from the time she spent there.

The photos of Madonna Fortin that Gary proceeded to reveal did show a different side to Madonna's mother. For one thing, Madonna Louise was a cheerleader. A cheerleader wearing a turtleneck, to be sure, but also a *front-row cheerleader*—the highest level on the cheerleader food chain, according to anyone who's ever gone to high school. Another photo, taken at a formal dance, showed three girls of whom Madonna Louise is distinctly the most beautiful and most elegantly dressed, with a big satin bow cinching her long, white dress and matching gloves—hardly the hair-shirted novitiate, at home with her bible.

Ex-boyfriend Jay Crete "remembers playing pool at parties in the Fortin basement," Gary continued, as snapshots taken by now-octogenarian childhood friends, many of whom he had personally tracked down and interviewed, scrolled across the screen. She was not, in the words of another ex-boyfriend, "overly pious" and enjoyed going to the popular Friday night dances held every week at St. James Gymnasium.

Gary's research in fact showed that the young Madonna Fortin bore a striking resemblance to her famously gregarious daughter. She was social, athletic, musical. She loved dancing and had a knack for leadership. She had a great sense of style and was clearly popular (the tagline under her photo reads, "She is wealthy in her friends"). And while we may never know if Madonna's mother ever showed the same signs of rebelliousness as her famous daughter, she did leave behind at least one poignant and highly unusual sign of self-assertion, a clue that Madonna's moxie might at least in part be an inheritance; she named her first-born daughter after herself. Even among Catholics it was a rare name; Madonna claims to have never met anyone else with the name other than her mother while growing up. And she has openly puzzled over her mother's uncommon choice. "Why would my mother name me after herself? My father didn't name *his* first son after him," she mused aloud in a 1994 interview with *Details* magazine. "It's almost like it's because, ultimately, I was going to be next. The only one."

Perhaps, as Madonna suggests, her mother already felt the shadow of death upon her and the name she gave her eldest daughter was a form of prophesy. Perhaps Madonna Fortin's tremendous faith simply outshone her modesty when it came to passing down the most exalted of names. But any way you look at it, it still was an extremely bold and anti-patriarchal move for a woman in Bay City, Michigan, to make in the year of 1958. Might one even call it . . . feministy? If it wasn't meant as a political goad, it still served as a personal one. Another thing Madonna once said about her name: "It feels like I have to live up to it."

"Madonna was no prude," Gary smiled, as a photo of Madonna Fortin and her friends lit up the screen behind him—the girls all lipsticked and roller-banged, the guys wearing loud shirts with pomaded hair, crowding a basement bar littered with beer bottles. "It's possible that Madonna Fortin upheld the grand tradition of St. Joesph's beer parties while in high school, and here's the photographic proof." The crowd laughed, and it wasn't just the intimation that Madonna's pious mother might have once actually had a beer in her life, but the whole humanizing picture of her family's extraordinary ordinariness that suddenly struck me. Amidst Madonna's relatives and her dead mother's friends, surrounded by people who may or may not have approved of Madonna, but who sat riveted by this glimpse of daily life on Smith Street, and their impresario, Gary Johnson, whose Rainmanlike determination to dig up these facts inspired no small degree of awe, I couldn't help but think Madonna would have liked to be here today. That she would have been honored, even moved, to see her own mother celebrated in her own hometown, regardless of what she really thought of Bay City.

"So where do we go from here?" Gary asked, having Power-Pointed through five decades of Madonna, during which she'd gone from a cherubic Communion girl, to a toned, waxed yogi whose face had begun to vacillate in ways impossible to ignore.

"I'm going to suggest a path that will require everyone in Bay City to open their hearts and embrace something that seems to have gone missing around here during this almost three-decades-long Madonna controversy," he intoned. Beat. "It's called forgiveness."

There was a lot to forgive: Tim Sullivan for denying Madonna her key, then exploiting that denial for political gain; Bay Citians for being too conservative and quick to condemn; ourselves for our ingrained prejudice against any young woman who has ever taken her clothes off for money; Madonna for being glib and often imperious; ourselves for shaming women who genu-inely, honestly, and unabashedly love sex; the *Bay City Times* for shoddy journalism back in 1987; and myself for instinctively dis-liking beautiful women who never quit and were unsurpassingly successful at the exact thing I had always wanted to do—the very thing I had tried and failed at.

"I know it will be difficult," Gary continued, "but I'm suggest-ing we should let these things from the past go and try to start anew. In that spirit, I think it would be wonderful if Bay City made the initial move. An obvious first step is to add 'Birthplace of Madonna' to the 'Welcome to Bay City' signs around town. This is not an honor," he added quickly. "We would be stating a fact. Bay City is the only place in the world that can make that claim. Most importantly, I would not tie either of these suggestions to Madonna having to attend the opening or the unveiling. Let's do it simply because it would be a generous thing to do." He paused for a moment. "And it would reflect nicely on Bay City."

The standing ovation that followed Gary's talk was jubilant, triumphant, epiphanic. And once the Q&A began, it became clear the entire room—and probably the hall outside, where an overflow crowd was watching on a wall monitor—was actually packed with Madonna fans who had been waiting a long time for this moment. There was the twenty-something male hospice nurse who had driven a hundred miles from Troy, Michigan, and local resident Nelson Brown, who proudly waved an 8 × 10 photo of the "Madonna shrine" he'd created in his basement, and a strongly pro-signage elderly woman who had been Madonna Louise Fortin's best friend in high school, and Jerry Charboneau, who brought Polaroids of the giant key he'd hand-tooled for Madonna after Mayor Sullivan snubbed her. A congressman had shown up, as well as two city council people. And Charles Brunner, the former mayor of Bay City, who added an addendum to the story of his effort to re-give Madonna the key to Bay City back in 2008. He had gone so far as to offer to drive out to Ford Field in Detroit, where Madonna was due to perform on her Sticky and Sweet Tour to deliver the key in person. And while Madonna's "people" politely declined (explaining she wouldn't have time for an onstage ceremony), he *was* offered two VIP tickets to the event. *Two VIP tickets!* Brunner sat down and an approving murmur went through the crowd. The mounting evidence seemed to suggest Madonna really *did* have great affection for Bay City, and maybe she hadn't haughtily ignored all of Bay City's strenuous apologizing. So when council member Chris Girard spontaneously stood up and declared that he would officially propose a Bay City "Birthplace of Madonna" sign at the very next city planning commission meeting, it came as no surprise to anyone. As the crowd poured out of that room, it seemed like anything was possible—even renaming Bay City itself "Madonnaland."

We piled into our frozen cars and headed over to Mavericks to celebrate. It was me, Gary, Ed Sierras, and a mysterious bearded man who attached himself to our party, explaining he knew exactly where Mavericks was because it was right near the city jail.

There we were greeted by a jubilant Marianna Super, who immediately fixed me a Madonna Latte (espresso, peppermint syrup, half a bag of sugar) and read my horoscope using a special chart where signs of the Zodiac had all been replaced by significant events in Madonna's life (Kaballah, Guy Richie, Super Bowl XLVI). Things got weird and sort of uncomfortable after that, when Marianna summoned a very blonde, very young girl with unspecified psychic powers to contact Madonna Louise Fortin from beyond the grave and get her read on her daughter's future prospects for signage in Bay City. Although the otherworldly prognosis for signage appeared to be good, Gary and I took this as our cue to leave.

Back when I still had a book to write, I had reserved a room in Bay City's historic Keswick Manor. Since I was told I would be the only guest in the hotel that night, I'd envisioned spending the evening kicking back with the proprietor as he regaled me with stories of Bay City's hundred-year history of shipbuilding, timber trading, and hell-raising. But Keswick's owner had gone north for the week to someplace even colder than Bay City, where, according to Chris, the college-student caretaker, the snowshoeing was better. So instead I got a one-sheet handout about Keswick's history to take up to my room. The mansion had been built at the turn of the last century by Robert E. Bousfield, who had run the Bousfield Woodenware Works, a company that built kegs and barrels, together with his brother. According to Keswick's proprietors, it was actually a Bousfield Barrel* that carried sixty-three-year-old Annie Edson Taylor successfully over Niagara Falls in 1901.

Alone in my high-ceilinged room, looking out at the dark, snow-covered houses lining Center Street, I began to feel conflicted about my role in turning the tide toward Madonna here. Was I helping to Disneyfy something historic and noble? I was certainly happy for Gary, but a touch sad for Annie Edson Taylor

---

*Others claim that it was actually the West Bay City Cooperage Company that Annie commissioned to build the barrel.

and Jacob Graverot and poor Ella Vaughn, a Bay City prostitute memorialized in wall text at the county museum for attempting suicide in jail by hanging herself with her skirt. A "Birthplace of Madonna" sign would quickly swamp their stories. Gary was right: Madonna being born here was the only thing that made Bay City interesting to the rest of the world. But it was no longer the only thing that made it interesting to me.

After I flew home to New York, however, I discovered an interesting bit of arcana that reaffirmed my support of Gary and the rest of the Madonna Underground.

Fifty-nine years after her death, Bay City finally decided to honor Annie Edson Taylor. In 1980, the president of the Bay City Chamber of Commerce, Frank Braman, tried to have Taylor's remains exhumed from the cemetery in Niagara Falls, New York, where she lay buried between two other Falls jumpers. His plan was to have the self-proclaimed Queen of the Mist's bones reinterred beneath a new memorial, a centerpiece tourist attraction for the Bay City boardwalk. A group called "Remaining Friends of Annie Taylor" fought back; Taylor's distant relatives were contacted, lawsuits were threatened, and her body was never moved.

Braman's macabre attempt to cash in on poor Annie Taylor's corpse made me feel considerably better; no matter how tacky a sign welcoming travelers to the city of Madonna's birth ended up being, nothing—*nothing!*—could be tackier than this. Two weeks later, Chris Girard's resolution "regarding signage marking the entrance to Bay City as the birthplace of Madonna using private funds" was unanimously approved by the Bay City Planning Commission, 7–0, and I couldn't help but notice Braman's argument for bringing the Queen of the Mist home to Bay City could just as easily apply to the Queen of Pop.

"She did something big, strong men fail at, and she did it on her own," Braman once said. "She's an amazing woman."

FIVE

MYSTERY OF THE MONDEGREEN, OR, WHO WAS THE FIRST BAND TO SMUGGLE THE WORD "MASTURBATE" ONTO THE BILLBOARD TOP 100?

After Gary's decathlon-level effort to enshrine Madonna in signage, I was surprised to learn that what he actually wanted that sign to say wasn't "Bay City: Birthplace of Madonna," but "Bay City: Birthplace of Madonna and '96 Tears.'"

"What's '96 Tears'?" I asked, confused.

"It's '96 Tears,' man!"

This, I soon learned, was the stock response of anyone familiar with the garage rock anthem to anyone who wasn't. The song "96 Tears" was written by the band Question Mark and the Mysterians in 1966, and behind its origin lay a classic American success story. It was here in Bay City that five sons of migrant farmworkers—most of them still teenagers—banged out a raw, catchy song in the home studio of a Russian hairdresser. Within months, "96 Tears" had catapulted to #1 on the Billboard charts. By the end of 1966, it ranked as the #5 song of the year, beating out Nancy Sinatra's "These Boots Are Made for Walkin'" (#13), the Rolling Stones' "Paint It Black" (#21), and the Beach Boys' "Sloop John B" (#61). The Mysterians became the first Mexican American rock band to achieve crossover success. They had also, sadly, peaked.

Personally, I found the possibility of a sign that compressed the vast spectrum of pop success to two such unlikely poles fascinating, but even Gary acknowledged that a "Birthplace of Madonna and '96 Tears'" sign was unlikely to pass muster with the Bay City Planning Commission; it was long, weird, and potentially accident-causing. So he conceived of a new municipal improvement plan: to ask Mayor Shannon to make "96 Tears" Bay City's official song. Four of the five original members of Question Mark and the Mysterians (including Question Mark himself) still lived in the area. Now in their late sixties, they continued to play local shows and record. Gary envisioned a nice award ceremony, a plaque, maybe a reunion concert at the historic State Theatre. After spending the better part of the year exiled in Madonnaland, I liked the idea of doing a story on a sexagenarian rock band that had blasted out of nowhere to graze the golden ring of rock stardom before descending, balloonlike, to live fairly normal lives. The news radio show I worked for agreed to send me to Bay City to cover the "96 Tears" Official Song story*—as long as Gary was successful in convincing the mayor.

From the get-go, the situation with "96 Tears" didn't appear nearly as bleak as it once had with the "Birthplace of Madonna" sign. In fact, when Gary approached Mayor Shannon about the idea, he seemed pretty amenable. But an unexpected question arose, one you'd think the mayor of Bay City himself best fit to answer: did Bay City *already* have an official song? Having lived in and

---

*By contrast, "Because, who cares about Madonna anymore?" was the rhetorical question posed to me by the NPR midwest bureau chief shortly before he rejected my pitch about the thirty-year struggle to put up a Madonna birthplace sign in Bay City. I wanted to point out that Madonna was the top-grossing celebrity of the previous year. That 114 million people watched her Superbowl Halftime Show in 2012 (a record high unsurpassed the following year by the mighty Beyoncé), and that one man, Robert Dewey Hoskins, was currently serving a ten-year jail term because he loved Madonna so much. (Hoskins was imprisoned for threatening to kill Madonna when she rejected his marriage proposal.) But I didn't say any of these things because I'd already been asked, "Who cares about Madonna?" so many times during the course of writing this book that sometimes it felt as though I was actually writing about Thigh Master or Koosh Balls or some other '80s relic rather than the most successful woman in rock history.

around Bay City his entire life, Gary had never heard of an official Bay City song; nonetheless, he took the question to Ron Bloomfield at the Bay County Historical Museum. The museum had no information about an official song either, but Bloomfield vaguely recalled something of the sort on record. It was only at the City Clerk's office that Gary finally succeeded in digging it up.

The song was called "Bay City Is Second to None," and it was written by Stewart Douglas and Wilson W. Hunt for a contest offering a cash prize run by the local paper. "Second to None" beat out thirty other entries for the prize, including "Now All Together for the 'Glad Hand' Town," "The Glad Hand Town," and "Old Glad Hand Town." (Apparently emphasizing Bay City's "glad hands" was not a winning strategy.) In mid-June of 1921, "Bay City Is Second to None" was heralded into life "by eighty business men," the *Bay City Times Tribune* reported, and proved "to have the rhythm and melody so needful if a song is to be remembered."

As far as I could tell, this was the last time anyone sang the official song of Bay City.

Surprisingly, news of the hard-to-locate song's existence put a chill on Mayor Shannon's enthusiasm. He told Gary that legally changing the official song would require a vote by the city commission, which he seemed to consider not worth the effort. The mayor instead suggested making "96 Tears" Bay City's official "rock and roll" song, which sounded like a nice gesture to me, but left Gary unmoved.

"After there's a Bay City Rock and Roll Song, what's next?" Gary railed. "An official Bay City Polka song? A salsa song? A rap?" He had nothing against these genres, he assured me, but it would dilute the honor. And "96 Tears" *deserved* to be Bay City's song. It was recorded right on Raymond Street. It was listed as one of the top five hundred greatest songs of all time by *Rolling Stone* magazine. The Rock and Roll Hall of Fame had declared it one of the "500 Songs that Shaped Rock." But there was another reason why Gary thought "96 Tears" should be Bay City's official song rather than "Bay City Is Second to None," one that had nothing to do with musical merit; he had dug up the original score and it turned out that the lyrics to "Bay City Is Second to None" were sort of . . . racist.

As one might assume from its name, "Bay City Is Second to None" was indeed a song about why Bay City was the best, a place where "the future is filled with promise" and "we all pull together as one." But then the authors go on to assert that Bay City is also "the place for the best of the race," which, lacking any reference to long-distance running, raises a giant red flag. Gary immediately fired off a message to Mayor Shannon.

"I am still holding on to the hope that you will reconsider your opinion regarding '96 Tears,'" he wrote. "I still fervently believe it should be given the higher honor of 'Bay City's Official Song.' I base this not only on the unique relationship '96 Tears' has to the city, but also on what now seems to be the somewhat questionable status of 'Bay City Is Second to None.'"

Unfortunately, it seemed the mayor had reached the end of his tether in terms of dealing with non-essential, rock-related inquiries. His reply to Gary's email conveyed he had more important city business to attend to, which, reading between the lines, might actually encompass *all* city business. I couldn't help but feel for Shannon; the mayorship of Bay City was an unpaid volunteer position. There was the trash collection and the budget to worry about, not to mention making sure all four of Bay City's drawbridges were manned around the clock during shipping season. Who knew how many other Garys were pestering Mayor Shannon about songs and signage?

Gary didn't see it that way. He couldn't understand Shannon's lack of attention to the Case of the Possibly Racist Official Song. I argued that Shannon had probably just skimmed over Gary's email due to the aforementioned more important city business, and failed to notice the thing about Bay City being "the place for the best of the race." Gary conceded this might be true, but then he began to wonder if there wasn't a more insidious reason Shannon was resisting the idea of making "96 Tears" the official song.

"Like what?" I asked.

"Like, you know . . ." Gary said, his voice thick with innuendo, "maybe the mayor knows the band originally intended to name that song '69 Tears.'"

I fell silent.

Sometimes I wondered about Gary.

The Mysterians were mysterious; it took me weeks, and multiple calls, to finally reach guitarist Bobby Balderrama, who "didn't believe in cell phones." But Question Mark had one-upped them by disappearing entirely. It had been more than a year since Question Mark (whose alleged birth name was Rudy Martinez) had played with the Mysterians, and he hadn't responded to Bobby's calls or emails about gig offers for months. Rumor had it the Mysterians had grown so frustrated with Que (as his friends called him) that last year keyboardist Frank Rodriguez—who had joined the band more than forty-five years ago—actually threatened to quit. This drama cast doubt on the question of whether Gary Johnson would even be able to assemble the original members for a victory lap if he did succeed in getting Shannon on his side.

While Gary worked on the mayor and the Mysterians worked on Question Mark, I decided to focus on Spanxing the band's fifty-plus-year history into some kind of coherent narrative. According to 96Tears.net, there were two documentaries about Question Mark and the Mysterians: guitarist Bobby Balderrama's *It's a Crazy World* and superfan Terry Murphy's *Are You for Real?* I was hopeful this surplus of footage would make my work much easier. But in place of the trailer for *It's a Crazy World* there was only a message reading "video stream not found." And the trailer for Murphy's film promised that *Are You for Real?* was "Coming Soon in 2011." So despite this frenzy of documenting, the band's website, festooned as it was with flashing GIFs, dead links, eBay memorabilia auctions, and donation solicitations, seemed less like a PR vehicle than an existential metaphor for something, like the subjective nature of knowledge. Every time I clicked on something and was rewarded by an actual fact, I half expected a crackerjack prize to fly out of some secret hole in my laptop.

At least the early part of the band's history was well known. Their story began in a basement in Saginaw in 1962, when drummer Robert Martinez, guitarist Bobby Balderrama, and his cousin, bassist Larry Borjas, first got together to jam. All three were the children of migrant farmworkers known as "Texicanos," pickers who traveled up from San Antonio to work the summer harvests in northern Michigan. In fact, it was in the strawberry fields of Standish, Michigan, that Bobby Balderrama got his first guitar lesson from a fellow picker. The opening of a General Motors plant in Saginaw, and the promise of steady, well-paying work, enabled their families to finally settle down for good. Once in school, the boys put together a nameless "three-piece thing." They played instrumental covers of songs by bands like the Ventures and booked gigs at any place that would have a Mexican American band.

As fate would have it, that same year Bobby and Larry happened to see a Japanese movie on television about an alien race that threatens to annihilate planet earth when they are denied a two-mile strip of land and unlimited access to human women. At first Bobby and the rest of the band were reluctant to go along with Larry's idea to name the band the Mysterians after the movie. (Paradoxically, their other idea lay at the opposite end of the ideological spectrum—to call themselves the Cadets and perform in full military garb.) But Larry prevailed, so they threw their aesthetic lot in with Japanese aliens wearing latex capes and matching motorcycle helmets. They had taken the first step on the path to Weird.

It turned out to be a two-step journey, the second and final step being Question Mark, whose name was still Rudy Martinez when he became the band's lead singer. Bobby Balderrama doesn't recall the teenage Rudy as being a particularly strange guy. "I don't remember any of that 'I was born on Jupiter stuff,'" he told me. "He was real quiet. Just a really nice guy."

But while there may not have been anything strange about Rudy before he became a Mysterian, he certainly emerged as maximally strange afterward. He would soon be claiming that his soul originated on Mars, that he built the pyramids and walked among the dinosaurs in a previous life. (His terrestrial history seemed to indicate he was born in 1945 and grew up in Michigan.) But the Mysterians didn't recruit Rudy because he was weird, or even because he could sing. Bobby's sisters had started coming home with stories about this kid tearing up the floor at local high school dances; the Mysterians' initial interest in Rudy was all about his hip action. But when they learned Rudy could also do a mean Mick Jagger impression, the Mysterians began banging out Rolling Stones covers. Rudy soon proved to be a charismatic and swoon-worthy frontman, and the Mysterians seemed assured a shining future on the northeast Michigan bar band circuit—until the Vietnam War intervened and Larry and Robert were drafted.

The change in lineup provided a transformative creative jolt, with the unlikely messenger of change being Larry's replacement, the tweenage Frank Rodriguez. Frank was only thirteen when he joined the Mysterians, but he'd been playing piano since he was five, which made him the musical veteran of the group. It was Rodriguez who came up with the maddeningly catchy, carnival-fairground riff of "96 Tears"—the da-da-da-da-da-da-dadee-dee-dee-dee-dee-dee-dee-dee Vox organ line familiar, yet distinct enough, to make anyone who swears that they've never heard "96 Tears" facepalm in immediate recognition upon hearing the first few bars. (Even though Question Mark got full songwriting credit for the song—as he did for most Mysterians' originals—strip away Rodriguez's Vox riff and all you have are some edgy lyrics and a bunch of wet eyes.)

The band recorded "96 Tears" in the home studio of Art Schiell, a Russian immigrant who worked as a hairdresser but devoted much of his free time to recording local bands, in April of 1966.* It was a low-fi setup. Bobby Balderrama remembers having to push a pool table out of the way to make room for the band. They tracked the song live, no overdubs; it took two hours and cost about $60. The single was immediately released on Pa-Go-Go Records, a Texas-based label with roots in the Mexican American migrant community.

At this point the band was still known simply as the Mysterians. It would be easy to imagine that the kind of guy who insists he was born 65 million years ago in outer space would also come up with the idea of calling himself Question Mark, and that's indeed what Question Mark himself has claimed. Then again, Question Mark also claims to have solved the mystery of the Shroud of Turin using his psychic abilities. Those who are not Question Mark say the idea was a marketing scheme thought up by the band's manager, Dave Torres. Torres assigned the other Mysterians stage names as well—letters of the alphabet X, Y, and Z—but as Balderrama told the *Chicago Reader* back in 1997, that didn't last long: "We were playing in Mount Holly, and I met this beautiful girl," Balderrama explained. "She goes, 'What's your name?' and I said, 'X.' She was like, 'God, this guy is weird.' So I had to give in to temptation, I guess."

Question Mark was the only one able to straight-facedly stick with his new name, er, symbol. To his credit, this gimmick

* In 2008, Gary also launched an effort to have a plaque placed in front of Art Schiell's former home on Raymond Street.

succeeded in getting the attention of the DJs at local radio station WSAM, whom Rudy and Bobby had been haranguing to give their new single a spin. (It also helped when they sent the station over one hundred fabricated postcards from "fans" requesting the song.) Before long the band was known as "Question Mark and the Mysterians."

The single quickly began charting in Saginaw, and then in Flint. When the Mysterians sold out of the first 750 copies of "96 Tears," Pa-Go-Go did a re-pressing and the band burned through the next 500 copies as well. Major labels began making offers, but the Mysterians ended up signing to the less well-known Cameo-Parkway label because their trademark color, orange, happened to be Question Mark's favorite. (If it helps explain what in retrospect turned out to be pretty poor judgment, "orange is more than Question Mark's color of choice," the Mysterians' website explains. "He is flat out maniacal about the vivacious and powerful hue.") In September of 1966, "96 Tears" debuted on the Billboard charts at #75. In October, it displaced the Monkees' "Last Train to Clarksville" as the #1 song in the country. Cameo-Parkway released their debut album, also called *96 Tears*. By November, it was certified gold.

Only seven months had passed since the band first stepped into Art Schiell's studio. They had gone from placing third in Bay City's "Battle of the Bands" to performing on Dick Clark's American Bandstand, opening for the Yardbirds, and touring with the Beach Boys. The rock jetstream had carried them from New York to Los Angeles. There were fans screaming for their autograph at record store signings and lines around the block when the band performed at Detroit's Cobo Hall, the same theater where Bobby had once seen the Rolling Stones perform. He remembers seeing that line and thinking to himself, "God, are we really playing here? Or is this a dream?"

Bobby Balderrama had just started tenth grade. Frank Rodriguez was still a freshman. That fall, Rudy Martinez legally changed his name to Question Mark. He walked into a car dealership in Flint, Michigan, and ordered a '66 Ford painted a custom orange for cash down. Not bad for a bunch of kids whose families had started off making $2.70 a day in the picking fields of the Saginaw Valley.

In their earliest photos, the band looks like a Mexican version of the Beatles, all shellacked hair and prep school clothes, nothing Mysterian about them except maybe Question Mark's ubiquitous shades. Not much was made of their Mexican roots. In the course of researching the band, I had more than one friend remark, "Oh, this story is just like 'Searching for Sugar Man,'" referring to the Academy Award–winning documentary about folk-rock troubadour Sixto Rodriguez. Yes, I'd reply, except the Mysterians were never rumored to be dead, weren't secretly famous in South Africa, and never wrote folk ballads about the plight of the working poor. Rodriguez and the Mysterians were both from Michigan and both active around the same time, but the connection everyone was referring to, of course, was their shared Latino heritage. The ease with which artists of such radically different sensibilities get tossed together only underscores the double-edged role that ethnicity can play in rock music. On the one hand, their Mexican heritage set Question Mark and the Mysterians apart from everyone else in an era when popular music was divided into "black" and "white." On the other hand, the Mysterians never *asked* to be set apart.

"I just think of us as a rock 'n' roll band," Question Mark told MusicScribe.com in 2008. "When you put on the radio all you hear is music. And you don't even know if there's females playin' music. And you don't even know if there's a crow playin' the music. You don't know what's playin' the music. All you know is that you hear music, right? And that's the way it should be."

I can't help but wonder if all of Question Mark's concerted weirdness—the shades, the punctuation fetish, the insistence on extra-terrestrial origins, the argument-starting claims of having invented the catchwords "hip," "cool," and "groo-vay"—is secretly an ingenious way of shutting down inevitable comparisons to Los Lobos or Rickie Valens or Sixto Rodriguez. By the time Question Mark was done being Question Mark, the very last thing a journalist would remember about him or the Mysterians was the color of their skin.

But as it turned out, not even the band's idiosyncrasies could save them.

Gary Johnson bristles when people call the band a "one-hit wonder," but it's at least accurate to call them a "number-one-hit wonder." "96 Tears" spent a week at #1. The follow-up "I Need Somebody" almost kissed the top 20, peaking at 22. Then came "Can't Get Enough of You Baby," a sound-alike forced on the band by their label, which withered at #56. (To today's ears, it sounds absurd—like someone took the keyboard line for "96 Tears" and spray-adhesived on new words, in the process hoovering out every bit of joy and spontaneity that made the original a hit. But bands ripping themselves off was such a common practice at the time that the listening public merely shrugged.)

Then came their controversial fourth make-or-break single, "Girl (You Captivate Me)." "Girl" barely broke the top 100, peaking at 98, which is too bad because of all the Mysterians' hit songs, to me, it is the most dynamic. Whereas the rat-a-tat-tat keyboard line of "96 Tears" keeps Question Mark's vocals boxed around a staccato melody, "Girl" finally gives him room to soar from a Michael Jacksonesque falsetto yowl to a Jim Morrisonlike purr.

The band's chart history ends with the catchy but forgettable "Do Something to Me," which failed to do much to anyone, sinking at 110. It was 1967. That same year, the no-longer-orange-labeled Cameo-Parkway would go bankrupt. The Mysterians' new label, Capitol Records, dropped them the following year after their first single failed to chart.

It was 1968 and most of the Mysterians were still in high school. The band soldiered on, but instead of hit songs, their plot now centered around lineup changes, failed-pseudonymous releases (as "The Semi-Colons and the Fun Sons"), and squabbles with management. Financially, the band was screwed, having signed away all their copyrights and ownership of their masters. The original lineup finally went their separate ways in 1969, but Question Mark formed a new group, without an organist, and kept performing. Then in 1997, promoter Jon Weiss helped convince the original band to re-form. Catching the garage rock resurgence, they toured the US and Europe before heading back to Michigan and resuming their 9–5 jobs as electricians, mechanics, manufacturing company employees, or in Question Mark's case, the occasional breeder of small dogs.

The thing is, there are hits and there are *hits*. The song "Winchester Cathedral," by the New Vaudeville Band (one of the only hit songs to ever prominently feature a bassoon, according to Wikipedia), actually spent three weeks at #1 on the Billboard charts in 1966 (as opposed to only one week, like "96 Tears"). It even won a Grammy. But you would be hard-pressed to find someone who could hum three bars of "Winchester Cathedral," whereas some of the greatest names in pop history have declared their enduring love for "96 Tears." David Bowie referred to the song as "an extraordinary piece of music." Dolly Parton is a life-long fan ("96 Tears" was the song playing the first time she and her future husband made love). Springsteen has covered the song numerous times live in concert, as have Aretha Franklin, Iggy Pop, and David Byrne. Tears remains in high-rotation on oldies stations and has been featured in commercials for Pringles and Honda (for which the band received no royalties). When I stopped to think about it, "96 Tears" was kind of the Madonna of one-hit wonders.

But not having been alive in the year 1966, I felt ill-equipped to answer the larger question of why this was so, and whether "96

Tears" had any deeper musical significance beyond the week it spent at the top of the charts in October of 1966. As a child of the '80s I could write a dissertation about how, say, John Waite's "Missing You" (a one-hit wonder from 1984) differed from similar synth pop ballads like Richard Marx's "Right Here Waiting for You" or REO Speedwagon's regrettable "Keep on Loving You." All were cheesy exemplars of the genre, true, but I could slice that cheese more finely than the finest deli slicer and would go to my death arguing that Waite was cave-aged Gruyère to REO Speedwagon's Velveeta. But when it came to separating the 1960s wheat from the chaff, I floundered.

"Cheesy, evil, roller-rink organ . . ." is how author and food-based-personality Anthony Bourdain described "96 Tears" during his guest DJ stint on KCRW. It was this song that first stoked his desire for a "rebellious drug-and-sex-drenched youth. ['96 Tears'] laid out for me the possibility for darkness in an otherwise happy landscape of AM radio pop music."

Reading Bourdain's words, I realized how hard it is—in an age when twerking is practically de rigueur and the only taboo in rock music that remains is the aural transmission of live, in-pasture, man-on-sheep sex—to imagine a cultural landscape in which Question Mark and the Mysterians could possibly be seen as disruptive. But to Bourdain in 1966, the Mysterians, with their "sinister" bowl haircuts and revenge-laced lyrics, were clearly a revelation, a necessary antidote to the turtlenecked boy-bands that crowded the radio dial. In 1968, when it made national news that Question Mark had been arrested by Michigan state police at a rest station off I-75 (along with an unidentified minor who may or may not have been Mysterian in origin) for glue sniffing, the band's trashy, ominous image grew exponentially trashier and more ominous. In an interview with NME magazine, Alan Vega, lead singer of the band Suicide, gave an un-politically correct ode to the band. Watching Question Mark and the Mysterians perform "96 Tears" on American Bandstand, Vega said "was like, holy shit for me. These five Mexican wetbacks in shades and black leather, junked out of their minds. The keyboard player was, like, fifteen. He was snortin' so much glue he couldn't even move his fingers. That song is, like, the National Anthem as far as I am concerned."

Vega's view of the Mysterians as dark, dangerous, and drug-addled may also help explain why a not insignificant number of influential rock critics have argued that "96 Tears" might just be the first punk song ever recorded.

Personally, I find punk an odd word to reach for when discussing the charisma of "Tears." Trying to pin a definition to a musical genre is like trying to nail a piece of wet soap to a wall, but if I were pressed to come up with the single defining characteristic of punk rock, I'd say that it's an *agitating* genre. Punk wants to make you nervous, whereas "96 Tears," though spare, is a song that wants to be loved. It's indulgent. It's got soul. To me it sounds like Motown—on meth.

But the theory that "96 Tears" was the world's first punk song has real legs. The very term "punk music" was actually coined in reference to Question Mark and the Mysterians. In the May 1971 issue of *CREEM* magazine, rock critic Dave Marsh described the band as "a landmark exposition of punk rock." This pronouncement wasn't a tossed-off hosanna, but rather marked a dramatic reversal of opinion for Marsh, who alongside fellow influential critics Lester Bangs and Greg Shaw had grown disenchanted with the increasingly cerebral and experimental leanings of mainstream rock.

"I used to hate groups like Question Mark and the Mysterians," Bangs wrote in one of a series of essays that ended up laying the theoretical groundwork for punk. "They seemed to represent everything simpleminded and dead-endish about rock in a time when groups like The Who and The Yardbirds were writing whole new chapters of musical prophecy almost daily."

But by the early '70s, these groups had fallen out of critical favor with the *CREEM* crew, fizzling "in an eclectic morass of confused experiments and bad judgments," according to Bangs, their music having grown "too good, too accomplished and cocky" to provide the visceral jolt that great rock music demands. The elevation of a bunch of all-but-forgotten garage rock bands of the previous decade marked a deliberate attempt on the part of these critics to bushwack a path through '70s progginess back to a purer, more adrenaline-based form of musical expression. According to Bernard Gendron, author of *Between Montmartre and the Mudd Club: Popular Music and the Avant-Garde*, Bangs, Marsh, and Shaw left no stone unturned in assembling the pantheon they would post facto define as the pioneers of punk.

"In their search for 1960s rock 'n' rollers who were neither touched by decadence, nor influential of it," Gendron explains, "Bangs and his allies searched through different makeshift categories—the British Invasion, surf music, American bands influenced by the British Invasion, such as the 'San Jose groups.' Gradually they settled upon a collection of not-well-known 1960s bands, one-hit wonders previously neglected by critics, who combined rank amateurism with a certain pugnacity—bands such as Count Five ('Psychotic Reaction'), The Seeds ('Pushing Too Hard'), and The Troggs ('Wild Thing'). Today we refer to them as 'garage bands,' but Shaw (or was it Marsh?) saw fit to name them 'punk bands,' a name that stuck."

This self-conscious act of rock history revisionism itself reads as too "accomplished and cocky" to be convincing; just because three *CREEM* critics felt The Who had gotten too pretentious doesn't retroactively make "96 Tears" the first punk song. That said, punk didn't just explode, magmalike, from the terra firma of '70s rock. It began as a series of musical cell mutations, a cancer on the bodies of sturdier predecessors. And garage rock, built on the dual piers of bombast and simplicity, is probably punk's closest relation. Maybe if we gave the Sex Pistols an Internet gene kit, we'd find that "Never Mind the Bollocks" was actually 5 percent Mysterian.

Regardless of whether it was the first punk song, first Latino rock hit, first *anything*, one phrase many critics and fans reach for in describing "96 Tears" is "ahead of its time." "Tears" was just a little darker, a little edgier, a little more raw-hearted than anything out there, as were the Mysterians themselves, who seemed to both mock and subvert the toothless, collegiate vibe of the times even while embracing it. But most of all, I think their mystique comes down to Question Mark and his tenacious weirdness. Since 1966, he has never shrugged off the name Question Mark. He has never once performed or been photographed without his trademark sunglasses. And he may even have been the only guy with enough cajones to smuggle the word "masturbate" into the Billboard top 100.

That was my theory, at least.

It's right there in the second line of the chorus to "Girl, You Captivate Me." "Girl, you captivate me," Question Mark sings. "Girl, you masturbate me."

Gary insisted there was no way Question Mark could have been singing the word "masturbate" on the radio in 1967, when less than a year earlier the Rolling Stones were forced to change the chorus of "Let's Spend the Night Together" to "Girl, let's spend some time together" in order to play the *Ed Sullivan Show*. Gary thought "Girl, you masturbate me" was a mondegreen (a misinterpreted song lyric) and that Question Mark was really singing "Girl, you *masticate* me."

At first I believed him. I went away and listened to the song maybe a dozen times—the last half-dozen with my husband. "OK . . . listen for it . . . Girl, you *masticate* me . . . next verse . . ." But each time the chorus came around Josh would look at me and go "I don't hear the 'cate.'" I didn't hear the "cate" either. I heard "bate." As in "masturbate."

The possibility certainly put the band's original title choice for "96 Tears"—"69 Tears"—in a whole new light.

"But masturbation means 'self-pleasuring,'" Gary protested when I told him his mondegreen theory wasn't holding water. "So to say that a girl is 'masturbating you' wouldn't make any sense!"

"Yes, but does it make any more sense to say a girl is 'masticating you?'" I asked. To which Gary could offer very little in response.

Even though "Girl, You Captivate Me" barely ticked into the Billboard top 100 at #98, if the word in question was really "masturbate," this would be quite an achievement. Gary was right: I mean, can you even think of any popular song before 1990 that includes the word "masturbate"? Not euphemistically, like "She Bop." Not spelling it out in so many words, like "when I think about you, I touch myself." I'm talking stone cold clinical. I'm talking masturbate. The only one I can come up with is Billy Joel's "Captain Jack," a song released five years after "Girl." But by 1973, the FCC was less dogged in its pursuit of the lyrically offensive. In the mid-'60s, even mild innuendo could get a single pulled. The song "Gloria" by the band Them (led by Van Morrison) was banned from WLS-FM in Chicago for the line, "She comes to my room, just about midnight" in 1966. And in 1967, The Who song "Pictures of Lily" was banned for merely alluding to masturbation, with lyrics like "pictures of Lily helped me feel alright."

A little more digging and I found what I believe to be the smoking gun: at a live show Question Mark recorded in Dallas in 1985, he announced to the crowd that the real title of "Girl, You Captivate Me" was actually "Girl, You Masturbate Me." Counter to Gary's belief, Question Mark clearly does embrace the idea of assisted masturbation. The real question is why Question Mark decided to go full frontal on the music censors back in 1967. Was he intentionally torpedoing his band's career, or was "masturbate" a last-ditch attempt to *save* the band—a publicity stunt deployed in hopes of keeping the band from sliding off the charts and into sad ignominy forever?

The Mysterians didn't even write "Girl, You Captivate Me." In an email, Bobby Balderrama explained the song was actually written by Joey DiFrancesco and Alan Dischel. Cameo-Parkway's vice president, Neil Bogart, had been the one who suggested they record it. Unsurprisingly, the original lyrics contained no reference to either masturbation or mastication:

> Girl, you captivate me
> I gotta tell you right now baby
> Girl, that's right—you fascinate me

Evidently Question Mark had changed the word "fascinate" to "masturbate," but how did he manage to get it past Cameo-Parkway and escape the FCC's ban on "outrageous" lyrical content?

I was excited to pose this question to Question Mark himself, but it was, unfortunately, seeming increasingly unlikely that I would get a chance to go back to Bay City to discuss masturbation. Gary hadn't made much headway with Mayor Shannon, although he had continued to research the story behind "Bay City Is Second to None." During our most recent chat, Gary had explained that the cover to the sheet music for "Second to None" referred to it as the city's "prize song."

"So?" I said.

"So if it's just the *prize* song of Bay City, not the *official* song, then there's no reason Shannon can't go ahead and make 'Tears' the official song. It shouldn't have to go to the city commission."

I kind of doubted this semantic argument was going to sway the mayor, but Gary told me he planned to scan the cover and send it over to Shannon anyway. I suggested he could also mention that a reporter for Public Radio International was working on a story about the fate of Bay City's official song.

Whether worn down by Gary's tenacity or motivated by the promise of press coverage, Shannon agreed to revisit the 96-Tears-as-Official-Song idea, and I called the mayor to set up an interview. I reached him on his cell as he was driving home from his non-mayoral job. Right away he told me that he had no intention of replacing "Bay City Is Second to None" and was only interested in making "96 Tears" Bay City's official "rock 'n' roll song." But besides the unwanted superlative, Gary would get everything he wanted: there would be a plaque, an official proclamation, and a performance featuring the original band lineup (with the exception of Eddie Serrato, who had died of a heart attack in 2011 and whose son would fill in as drummer) at Old City Hall, a popular local restaurant and club.

I asked the mayor why he had decided to stand by "Bay City Is Second to None." "'Tears' is a great song," Shannon said, "but it's also a song about a guy crying his eyes out because his lover left him—not exactly something you want as your national anthem."

Perhaps not, I conceded, but what about the racist lyric in "Second to None"?

There was a long pause, during which I could practically hear the wind in Mayor Shannon's car windows as the exurban paysage of M-25 scrolled by.

"What lyric?" he said.

As I'd suspected, Shannon hadn't read through all of Gary's messages; this was the first he'd heard about Bay City being "the place for the best of the race." Before we got off the phone, he promised to give the issue a second look.

While the mayor began to contemplate who Bay City was really the best place for, I continued to fail to reach Question Mark. After three weeks of effort, I succeeded in finally getting a solitary email response with a cell number, only to learn that Question Mark never answers his phone. So in lieu of actually questioning Question Mark, I sat in front of YouTube and watched as he picked through the burnt debris of his house.

After their short Billboard chart run ended, the Mysterians resumed their civilian lives. Bobby went to college and became an electronic technician. Frank Rodriguez found work as a mechanic servicing industrial machinery. Bassist Frank Lugo got a job at General Motors. Only Eddie Serrato maintained a career in music, working for a span as an engineer at Joey Records, a Tejano label based in San Antonio.

After a stint in California, Question Mark returned to Michigan. He moved in with his longtime manager, Luverne Thompson, and Thompson's wife, who owned a house outside of Flint in the town of Clio, and set up a small dog-breeding business. On January 7, 2009, the house burned to the ground, sparked by a faulty electric socket. It was the dogs, not the forty years of memorabilia, that Question Mark mourned. Four of his Yorkies died in the fire before Question Mark could reach them, together with his prized cockatoo. The three Yorkies he did manage to save all ended up dying before the end of the year. In the video he made to solicit donations, his voice quavers as he scans the charred rubble and talks about searching for his dogs' bodies. But suddenly he remembers his public and turns stoic. "I won't be on the bottom for long," he promises the camera. "I don't cry tears, I sing them."

Without insurance, Question Mark and the Thompsons had no money to rebuild. The fire was covered on the local news, and Question Mark put an appeal on YouTube directing fans to a PayPal account. He moved into a single-wide trailer on a rural lot he shared with a menagerie of pigs, chickens, cows, and various car carcasses. Six months after the fire, he made another YouTube video advertising that the Mysterians' tour bus was for sale for $69,000 (reference to "96 Tears": intentional). The video shows Question Mark in high spirits. Though the sunglasses remain, the gaunt dude with the bowl cut is long gone. This new incarnation of Question Mark has dropped the long-sleeved shirts and the trench coat. His signature locks have been replaced by a shoulder-length wig, and he now favors frilled women's blouses, left unbuttoned and knotted over his midriff, and very tight, high-waisted pants. (His midriff, by the way, is *legit*.) With his Vegas showgirl attire and long dark hair, Que is decidedly more Hedwig, less McCartney.

After providing a tour of the bus, he does a little dance in his fringed leather jacket. There is a bizarre segue where he announces a return to "our feature film: *Gone with the Wind*," and suddenly Question Mark is down on all fours, clawing through the chunky soot where his house once stood, moaning, "I've got to find my gold record! I've got to find my gold record!" The video's aesthetic falls somewhere in the territory between performance art and a QVC infomercial.

The last video in the Question-Mark-house-fire series went up in 2010 and shows Question Mark walking around what may someday be his new home, but for the moment remains a plywood box in waterproof sheathing. There has been no news since then of the house's completion, and I wonder where the phone I am calling is actually ringing. Gary tells me that Bobby Balderrama, who has left several messages for Question Mark regarding the upcoming Bay City concert and the whole official-rock-song-of-Bay-City thing, hasn't heard back and is wondering whether Que might be ill.

But once the venue is booked, the date is set, and it becomes clear the remainder of the Mysterians are determined to play the Official Rock Song concert with or without Question Mark, he finally starts returning my calls. And once he starts calling me, he doesn't stop.

Question Mark, I soon discover, is upset about everything. He is upset about the way things are being handled in Bay City. He is upset with his bandmates for giving "unauthorized" interviews to the *Bay City Times*. He is upset with Mayor Shannon for booking a venue he considers too small. More generally, he is upset with the world for not paying more attention to him. He leaves messages asking me to call him back after *Dancing with the Stars* is over, then spends half the conversation railing against other performers, also-rans like the Rolling Stones, Bob Dylan, and "Lady Kaka." Later, I learned he had turned his knack for criticism into a sideline, serving as a supplementary Simon Cowell for a Saginaw radio show's weekly *American Idol* recaps. "He's had three different hairstyles in three weeks," Question Mark railed against teen-heartthrob contestant Sanjaya Malakar in 2008. "That's three more than his styles of singing, which is zero."

I start to find dealing with Question Mark's surfeit of dissatisfaction exhausting; before long I've gone from pining for a callback to seeing his number on my cell and quietly pocketing it. Then Question Mark goes after Gary—or rather, his publicist, a Mysterians uber-fan named Susie, goes after Gary—to expunge all references to the name "Rudy Martinez" from Gary's blog. "Rudy Martinez" was not Question Mark's real name, the publicist maintained. In fact, "Question Mark" wasn't Question Mark's real name. His real name was "?," and Gary's misrepresentation, the publicist alleged, was causing real suffering to the Rudy Martinezes of Michigan, who were having to deal with a lot of disappointed Question Mark fans showing up on their doorsteps. The Question Mark team also objected to Gary's assertion that Que had attended Saginaw High School. In addition to wanting all references to "Rudy Martinez" and "R. Martinez" removed from his blog, they insisted he delete any references to Saginaw High.*

You do not want to get into a fact-checking competition with Gary Johnson, I wanted to tell Question Mark; he will drive farther and out-microfiche you. He will crush you with the brute force of his archival research. Which is exactly what Gary did,

---

* Later, after my piece aired, Question Mark's publicist called my editor at PRI to demand that all the "Question Marks" in the piece be changed to "?s" and that we remove any reference to the word "Latino" (because there is no such country as "Latino") as well as the phrase "one-hit wonder" because the Mysterians charted five times between 1966 and 1967, if you count "Do Something to Me," which peaked at #110.

first by calmly pointing out that R. Martinez was the name that appeared in the songwriting credits of all the old Mysterians records. And then by getting into his car, driving to Saginaw, and digging up Saginaw High School yearbooks from the years 1960, 1961, and 1962. Later he sent me scans of Rudy Martinez's yearbook photos, all of which bore a strong resemblance to the young Question Mark, as well as a copy of a Saginaw newspaper article from April 3, 1968, about the infamous glue-sniffing arrest that included the line, "Rudy Martinez, 23, of 820 Howard identifies himself as Question Mark."

I hadn't even left New York and I was already exhausted by Question Mark, who had undoubtedly found some reason to dislike me by now. I could only conclude that being a (#1) hit wonder does something to you. Perhaps it's like the decompression sickness divers experience when they ascend too high too fast. The issue of what exactly it does to you, however, is not a topic most one-hit wonders are interested in broaching with a journalist. This hunch was affirmed for me when I stumbled upon the transcript of an aborted interview with my favorite number-one-hit-wonder of the '80s: John Waite. It was conducted by journalist Mike Ross in 2012 with the express aim of exploring "the phenomenon of massive hit songs becoming so well known that they actually dwarf their creators."

Q: First of all, does the term "one-hit wonder" offend?

JW: If I was a one-hit wonder, it probably would. That would relegate me to a certain time period and that would just be hello and goodbye. But the Babys had some gigantic records, I've had a No. 1 with Bad English, No. 1 as a solo. I just had a No. 1 record on the radio last year with "Rough and Tumble."* You can look at it in relative terms—what's bigger than what else I've done? There's been quite a few No. 1s, really.

---

* "Rough and Tumble" charted as #1 on the Classic Rock radio chart, not the mainstream Billboard charts.

Q: But "Missing You" was EVERYWHERE. It was such a big song all over the world. People who never listen to music would know the song and wouldn't even know who you are. What do you think? Do you think these types of songs can become more famous than their creators?

JW: I have no idea how to reply to that.

Q: Well, there was Deep Purple and "Smoke on the Water"; the guy said the song seemed to take on a life of its own. And Don McLean . . .

JW: Who's he? Never heard of him . . .

Q: Ha, ha, well, he had a troubled relationship with "American Pie," as if it became a Frankenstein monster or something . . .

JW: I consider myself to be way ahead of that one, but this seems to be something you want to approach as a derogatory thing.

Q: Why is it considered derogatory?

JW: It's like, do you want to do an interview or you really don't? Because, man, I've got better things to do than this shit.

Q: I understand, but . . .

JW: I'm really serious.

Q: You are offended.

JW: I'm not offended! If you read me like that, then what the fuck are we talking for?

Q: I'm not . . .

JW: Tell you what. Nice talking to you. See you down the line. Bye, bye . . . (click)

I feared that something similar would happen between me and Question Mark; I would ask him a few sensitive questions and off-the-handle he would go, scotching the entire event and all of Gary's hard work. And yet when I arrived in Bay City on August 14 for the mayor's official proclamation, the Question Mark who greeted me was not the man I expected. I had steeled myself for a half-hour of self-aggrandizement and unfiltered defensiveness, but found Que oddly subdued, even humble. Even though he was cloaked in a cowboy hat, wig, and sunglasses, his age showed. The lines on his face were deeply etched, his dental work sketchy. I asked where he'd been born, expecting to hear "Mars" or to be told that places didn't even *have* names ten thousand years ago. But he simply said he'd been born in Michigan, "on some dirt road." I asked how his new house was coming along. "Bad," he replied. Four years later, the house was still just a shell.

"We're poor," Question Mark continued. "I mean, we're broke. And I advertise that on my Facebook. Like B.R.O.K.E. in capital letters. Yeah."

Then he spelled out the names of the websites where he accepted donations.

He did, of course, reiterate his belief that "rock 'n' roll died" after "96 Tears." While his bandmates seemed to be done dining at the buffet of "96 Tears"—the Mysterians had put together a different band called the Robert Lee Revue whose new single, "Happy & Go Lucky," was currently #22 on the Mediabase Smooth Jazz Chart—Question Mark announced he was planning to release *three* new versions of "96 Tears" in the coming year, including one in Spanish.

The weird thing was that despite his apostolic faith in the power and longevity of "96 Tears," Question Mark had made it a policy to never discuss the inspiration behind its lyrics.

"Somebody said, 'What are your songs about?'" he told me, "and I felt like saying, 'Huh, really?' Listen to the lyrics! They're about life. People can take the words however they wanna take it and whatever it means." He paused. Then added, "But my IQ is 425."

Speaking of lyrics-about-life, I thought to myself and blurted the question I'd been waiting to ask: why had he changed the words "Girl, you fascinate me" to "Girl, you masturbate me" back in 1967?

"I like the edge," Question Mark said, unphased by the abrupt change in topic. "Because I'm a writer. Only if you really feel that the word should be used—any kinds of cuss words, adult words—then you use those words because that's what life is all about. And I really felt they're talking about foreplay and so why not just come out and say, 'You fascinate me, you captivate me, and you masturbate me?'" In fact, Question Mark explained, he'd actually gone much further in his quest for edgy truth. At the end of the B-side, "Love You Baby (Like Nobody's Business)," Question Mark said, "We say, 'We don't smoke, we don't drink, nor fuuuck.'" And this was 1968, Question Mark added proudly, "before Country Joe and the Fish said it at Woodstock."

Later, guitarist Bobby Balderrama wrote to tell me that not everyone in the band was happy with Question Mark's decision to change the "Girl" lyrics, but by then they were already having serious legal issues with their label, Cameo-Parkway, and had bigger things to worry about.

So now I had my answer: Question Mark had probably been the first guy to smuggle the words "masturbate" and "fuck" onto commercial radio. When I thought about it, there was an eerie parallel here between Question Mark and Madonna, who not only sang about these things but simulated them live. But Madonna's videos were condemned by conservatives and her concerts boycotted because of it, fanning the inferno of her fame ever higher. Whereas in Question Mark's case, no one seemed to care. Not Cameo-Parkway. Not the radio stations. Not the FCC.

Just me. And Gary Johnson.

A half-hour later, Mayor Chris Shannon officially declared "96 Tears" to be the Official Rock 'n' Roll Song of Bay City, while outside, fans wearing black T-shirts punctuated with neon orange question marks pressed their faces against the pane glass window. Ultimately, the mayor had stuck by his decision to keep "Bay City Is Second to None" as the city's official song. He told me that he preferred to believe that when the authors described "Bay City as the place for the best of the race," it was the human race they were referring to and not, you know, white people. The lyrics should be interpreted through "the lens of time," he explained when we spoke in the loudly ventilated dressing room of Old City Hall just before Question Mark and the Mysterians were due to perform, and "should be remembered as part of [Bay City] history."

"I know people may disagree with me, like Gary Johnson," the mayor smiled, "but that's OK."

Neither the fans who had flown in from as far away as Alabama and driven from as far as Kentucky, nor the band itself, seemed to feel that the Mysterians' honor had been somehow besmirched by the "rock 'n' roll" qualifier. Question Mark sang four songs with the Mysterians; two of them were "96 Tears." Both times the band played it, the crowd went wild. Sadly Gary, who was spending the month with his grandchildren in New Jersey, wasn't there to see it. The Mysterians were still tight and Question Mark could still throw it down. He rolled on the floor, shimmied through the aisles, jumped in the air. The rest of the Mysterians rocked on the balls of their feet, buzzed and grinning. Time receded; their age felt insignificant, a meaningless number. And as the audience held their glowing cell phones aloft, I could see a hundred tiny Question Marks dancing on their LCD screens, ecstatic to have finally reached that elusive place where "Tears" could live on forever.

SIX

FLYING WEDGE,

OR, COULD A BAND WITH THREE FANS BE

(ANOTHER) MISSING LINK BETWEEN

HARD ROCK AND PUNK?

It started when I was down in Nashville with my friend Allyson to interview Ben Blackwell, supervisor of vinyl production at Jack White's Third Man Records (his official job title is "pinball wizard") for a story that ultimately went nowhere. Ben grew up in Detroit and for seven years ran his own label, Cass Records, which he launched from the bedroom of his childhood home after dropping out of college. During the course of our interview he happened to mention he was an avid collector of Michigan rock, especially rare vinyl. So I told Blackwell that I was heading up to Michigan to interview Question Mark and the Mysterians in a few weeks and, on a whim, asked if there were any rock 'n' roll stories—perhaps a great mystery in the vein of *Searching for Sugar Man* or *A Band Called Death*—still lurking in Motor City. Ben considered this question for what seemed like a long time. Then he said two words: Flying Wedge.

I wrote them down on my hand.

Once back in New York, I discovered that Flying Wedge was possibly the coldest rock 'n' roll case ever. In fact, what little could be gleaned online about the band mostly came from interviews with Blackwell himself. Flying Wedge's output, as Blackwell explained in an email, consisted of "a lone self-released 7-inch, heavily sweated by collectors." And by "collectors," he meant about three people. "I Can't Believe," one of the songs from the Flying Wedge single, was posted on YouTube in August of 2012; almost two years later it had only notched 528 views.

The gist of the story according to Blackwell was this: sometime in 1972, a bunch of very young black guys walked into the offices of *CREEM* magazine and handed then-editor Ben Edmonds their newly pressed single. They didn't leave their names, nor was there any information about the band on the record itself save for the names of the songs—"I Can't Believe" and "Come to My Casbah"—and the name of the label, Brown Whole Jams. Edmonds took the record home and played it; what he heard blew his mind. But with scant information about the band or the record, he had nothing to write about. So he gave the record to his housemate, Dan Carlyle, a DJ with an evening show on WABX, Detroit's underground rock FM station. Like Edmonds, Carlyle was stunned by the two tracks and immediately declared the band the "Black Stooges."

For an entire week, Carlyle played the record every night. And each time he beseeched the band, and his audience—really anyone who knew of Flying Wedge—to call him. The phone never rang. So Carlyle stopped playing the record, and soon after, the 7-inch, Edmonds's only copy, disappeared from the WABX library. For the next forty years, Edmonds trolled local record shops, asking vinyl hounds if they'd ever heard of the band Flying Wedge. It got to the point, Edmonds confessed, where he almost thought he'd imagined the whole thing. Until one day his friend Ben Blackwell sent him *Michigan Meltdown*, a vinyl compilation of rare Michigan rock. To Edmonds's surprise, there at the end of side two were the Flying Wedge songs from the long-lost single.

Blackwell actually had no idea Edmonds had ever heard of the band, let alone once met them—he had first learned of Flying Wedge from another collector of rare Michigan vinyl, Brad Hales, owner of Peoples Records in Detroit. It was at a party at Hales's place sometime in 2010 that Blackwell pulled the Flying Wedge single out of a box. The artwork on the label was what attracted him at first.

"It just looked so wrong and primitive," Blackwell recalls, "like some teenager scrawled it in a spiral bound notebook or something." But like Edmonds, he was also immediately struck by what lay between the grooves. The music was eerily unplaceable. "It could have been made in 1969 or '79 or '89." These were the kind of records that excited him the most: the ones that sounded as though they'd been made in a vacuum.

"Forget about Black Merda. Forget about Parliament. Forget about Death," Edmonds told Blackwell after receiving *Michigan Meltdown*. Flying Wedge was "the pinnacle of Black Rock."

Like the Hackney brothers, who comprised the proto-punk band Death, Flying Wedge was unusual in that they were an African American band playing heavy rock in both an era and a city where Motown reigned. But the band Death was never as invisible as Flying Wedge. Death's recording sessions were paid for by Clive Davis, president of Columbia Records. Flying Wedge's sole release was obviously a DIY job. And the members of Death, unlike the members of Flying Wedge, were not hard to track down. Their latter incarnation, a reggae band called Lambsbread, went on to release eight albums. Before either the 2009 *New York Times* article "Death Was Punk before Punk Was Punk" or the 2013 documentary about the group, *A Band Called Death,* announced their existence to the world, Ben Blackwell (who later appeared in that documentary) had already approached the surviving members of Death about the possibility of reissuing their music.

Given the void of information about Flying Wedge, I decided to circle back to Edmonds (now the US correspondent for *MOJO*) to get his firsthand impressions of the band and their music, hoping for some clue as to their whereabouts.

"It seemed to me like they were messing around with rock 'n' roll ideas that were a little more pure than Black Merda, or Death, or Parliament Funkadelic for that matter," Edmonds told me. "It was the best piece of noise I had heard in quite a while, especially coming from such an unlikely source. The kids were just kind of shy and looking around, and they kind of pushed the record toward me and then were gone. I don't really remember talking to them about anything. But when I listened to it, I heard just this wonderful, wonderful rock 'n' roll noise."

The intervening years didn't change his opinion. When he heard the two tracks on *Michigan Meltdown* the music "sounded pretty much to me like it did back in '72 or '73. Like the wonderful beginning of something that it doesn't sound like it ever progressed beyond this, but what a wonderful beginning it was."

I couldn't help but wonder, though, how much the fact that Edmonds knew the band was black had influenced his impression of the music. If the Flying Wedge single had just arrived in the mail, or if a bunch of white, affluent college kids had arrived in his office and dropped the single on his desk, would he have had the same reaction? On the phone, Edmonds insisted it wouldn't have made any difference to him if the band had been white. But a few weeks later he shot me the following mea culpa:

I think I gave you some lame pc answer about how [the Flying Wedge single] would have been interesting wherever it came from. Of course the truth is that it was of interest primarily because it was a black record. A black record that didn't appear to contain any of the customary black music reference points. It was obviously infused with rock & roll energy, but wasn't aping anything on the rock side either. This is where the Stooges comparison comes in. The Stooges invented themselves out of nothing, rock's first great DIY story. Though the drummer of Flying Wedge has obviously had some experience, the overall sound is of a band inventing itself on the spot.

What really intrigues me is what this record says about the city at that moment in time. With all the archaeological dig work that's been done, we can see a much more vibrant "black rock" (hate that term) scene than any of us imagined. It existed at all levels: from George Clinton, who successfully forged an alliance with the underground rock scene, to Black Merda, who put out records but were never able to make Clinton's connections, to Death, who made an album but wouldn't play ball with the industry, to Flying Wedge, who made a mysterious 45 oozing with personality and then disappeared. What's especially interesting is how little awareness each of these developments had of each other. Without any base of support in the black community, most never got out of their neighborhoods. And what might have been going on in other neighborhoods? There's probably a book in there, with one hell of a soundtrack album.

But Edmonds also cautioned me not to read too much into the significance of Flying Wedge. "I hesitate to give you a 'this is the greatest thing' kind of record-collector bullshit, because it's not that," he said. "For example, Dan played [the single] on WABX for a week, but if it had potential to go beyond that and become a hit, or even a more widely played record, other DJs at the station would have picked it up and played it as well and nobody else did. It remained Dan's private passion. This is an interesting curio, but it's not like we could make it out to be the second coming of anything. Or the first coming of anything."

Despite Edmonds's warning, I remained hooked on the idea of finding Flying Wedge. Their case posed an intriguing question: if a band makes music history in their bedroom but no one is there to hear it, have they truly made music history? Reason says the answer must be no; after all, these bands had no influence, either musically or culturally, on anything that followed. But couldn't there be a paleontological, Lucy-like significance to such a find? One that would prove that taken as a species, rock and rollers were more musically evolved earlier than we suspected? Or to quote some wall text I saw at the Bay County Historical Museum credited to William R. McCormick, an early settler, "The pioneer's name never shines among the brilliant and illustrious names on the history page. He is only a path finder, carrying the torch of discovery into the Wilderness; yet without him civilization is impossible."

Besides, if the members of Flying Wedge could be found, and the full body of their music brought to light, then who was to say it was too late for the band to make an impact? After all, the task of piecing together rock and roll's genesis—the elusive "big bang" when rhythm and blues became rock, or rock became punk, or metal, or New Wave, or rap—is a largely retroactive one. There is nothing rock historians love more than a good old-fashioned truffle hunt. After decades of obscurity, Sixto Rodriguez's two "lost" albums from the '70s (which unbeknownst to him provided the sound track for white South Africa's anti-apartheid movement) have now been added to the canon of American folk music. At age seventy, he played the Glastonbury Festival to an audience of almost 120,000 people. Similarly forgotten, the band Death is now being hailed as the "missing link" between garage rock and punk, with a new album out on the ur-hip Chicago label Drag City. So I couldn't help but look toward the vague outlines of the Flying Wedge story and wonder whether, as the saying goes, there was also *gold in them thar hills*. It was true that the band only had three American fans (so far as I could see), but those fans were an august group: Edmonds, the former editor of

CREEM; Blackwell, who helped run one of the most successful vinyl labels in the country; and Hales, who in addition to owning Peoples Records had just created the Michigan Audio Heritage Society Museum in Detroit. And there was a lurking feeling among them that Flying Wedge was simply too musically evolved to have only recorded two songs.

On the other had, the opposing scenario—that there was really nothing more to Flying Wedge than one odd single—held its own fatalistic appeal. Rodriguez without South Africa. Death without its cult following in the San Francisco punk scene. What if the story of Flying Wedge was the story of a band that didn't have the time, money, patience, or luck, or were never predisposed by character or circumstance to Sherpa their music out of obscurity? These kinds of stories were legion but rarely told, because they didn't have a real ending or a satisfying arc. Just a long string of disappointments followed by acquiescence, whether gradual or sudden, reluctant or whole-hearted. Then: silence.

I decided to send a note to my favorite rock-based detective, Gary Johnson, asking if he knew anything about Flying Wedge. He didn't. But Gary did tell me that if the band was active in Detroit in the '70s, they likely had their 7-inch manufactured at Archer. Archer was legendary in Detroit for being a color-blind plant where any musician could literally walk in the door and get their music pressed. I contacted Archer and to my surprise they got back to me right away, asking for the matrix numbers on the single. (A matrix number is the number scribed between the end of the last track on an album and the beginning of the label.) Excitedly, I sent a note to Ben Blackwell, and just as fast, Blackwell told me not to bother with Archer. He used to work at the plant back when he lived in Detroit and had personally gone through all of the invoices for the relevant years himself by hand; Archer had no record of Flying Wedge. I got on the phone with Blackwell and it soon became clear that he knew a lot more about the band than he'd originally let on. He knew that their label, Brown Whole Jams, had pressed some music at Archer and some at QCA in Cincinnati. He knew that Rob Sevier at Numero Records (a prestigious reissue label based in Chicago) had been looking for the group, and might know something of their whereabouts. But the biggest bombshell was that a few months ago, Brad Hales had told Blackwell that a guy walked into Peoples Records and mentioned he was once a member of Flying Wedge. The guy promised to come back to the shop to consign some Flying Wedge singles, but never did.

I wondered why Ben, whose interest in the band was intense enough that he would personally comb through the Archer archives in search of ancient receipts, hadn't followed up on any of these strong leads himself. If he knew QCA might still have some original recordings on file, why hadn't he checked with them? Ben's explanation was that he doubted QCA would go through their archives just because he asked. (An answer I found fairly unconvincing.) And when I asked why he wasn't trying to get more info from Rob Sevier and Brad Hales, both more than passing acquaintances of his, I got a speech that I would eventually hear from every vinyl hunter involved in the Flying Wedge story: "Don't get me wrong, I love _____, he's one of my best friends. But the thing you have to understand about certain record-collector types is they tend to play things pretty close to the vest. And _____ just happens to be one of those guys." Ben never did explain why he didn't share any of this information with me earlier, but he did give me one more vital clue before we got off the phone: the Flying Wedge single credited the album artwork to someone named Corbin.

I decided to start by contacting QCA. Even though it was the most remote of the leads Ben had given me, it was also the likeliest to yield new, unreleased music by Flying Wedge. As it turned out, Jim Bosken, QCA's president, was immediately helpful.

Unlike Archer, QCA had retained the majority of its records—job files, customer cards, and most alluringly, *original lathe cuts*. I gave Jim the matrix numbers from a Brown Whole Jams single that Ben had identified as a QCA pressing. (It wasn't the Flying Wedge single, but we hoped that more information about the label would lead to more information about the band.) Jim got back to me just a few hours later. What was known about Brown Whole Jams' output had just doubled.

The first job QCA did for Brown Whole Jams was five hundred units of a single called "Jettin Around" by a band called "Miraculous." It was never re-pressed. The second job was a much smaller run: one hundred units of another 7-inch with two tracks titled "Space Lady" and "Those Sweet Memories." The last job QCA did for the label was a reference acetate—just one lathe cut—for a single called "Get My Love" that was never pressed. The good news was that QCA had retained the master tapes for the latter two singles. The bad news was that all of these records were pressed in 1982—ten full years after Flying Wedge walked into the *CREEM* offices—and none were recorded by the band I was looking for. However, there was a name associated with the account, and that name matched the album art credit on Ben's Flying Wedge single; all the Brown Whole Jams orders had been made by Greg Corbin, with an address listed in Detroit.

Having some Flying Wedge currency of my own to bring to the table emboldened me to call the next Michigan rock expert on my list, Brad Hales. Hales confirmed that a few months ago a member of Flying Wedge had wandered into Peoples and they'd struck up a conversation. My heart quickened a little.

"Was his name Greg Corbin?"

"Greg Corbin is dead," Hales said.

It was Greg's brother Matt, Hales explained, who had dropped by Peoples. "He left his card," he added. Then I listened in disbelief as Hales rummaged through a drawer on the other end.

Suddenly I was writing down Matt Corbin's number.

By now the mystery of Ben Blackwell was starting to dwarf the mystery of Flying Wedge—it beggared belief to think that Ben didn't know Hales had been sitting on Matt Corbin's number for months. I shot Blackwell a one-line note: have you been holding out on me, Ben? His one-line reply came back right away: "Of course I'm holding out."

Whereas the Internet remained all but mute on the subject of Flying Wedge, searching Matt Corbin's name immediately called up something interesting, an entry on a work titled *Geome Tree* from a book by Dennis Nawrocki about public art in Detroit.

Geome Tree was a series of sculptures Corbin had built, along with another Detroit artist, fashioned from salvaged materials and industrial detritus around an Egyptian theme. The permanent installation included an "obelisk" made from a thirty-five-foot abandoned crane, "temple columns" fashioned from concrete sewer pipes, and "a rotating arrow on a tripod base, a sundial, a circular well, and two low-lying pyramids." According to the author, Corbin was born in 1945, studied at Detroit's College for Creative Studies, and now worked as a sculptor and teacher. The other interesting thing I noted was the location: *Geome Tree* was built on a vacant lot on the corner of Clairmount Street and Second Avenue in downtown Detroit. The house across the street from that lot was the address listed on Greg Corbin's QCA job orders.

While there was no guarantee that the story of Flying Wedge would be an interesting one, the presence of pyramids and the specter of Greg Corbin's death made it seem more likely.

I picked up the phone and gave Matt Corbin a call.

The ceiling of Matt Corbin's living room is fringed with funeral programs, each dangling from a single pin, circling the room like pom-poms on a sombrero. He calls this the "Room of Spirits."

There must be at least a hundred of them, bull's-eyed with Xeroxed faces of the newly dead. Actually the funeral programs are everywhere—fanning out from napkin holders, coastering side tables, propped up like guests on the seats of overstuffed armchairs. Matt Corbin gets up on a chair and takes one of the programs down from the wall, handing it to me. The photograph is of a handsome, goateed black man, his hair combed over to one side to form a thick braid. "A Service Celebrating the Life of Gregory Joseph Corbin. August 14, 1999," it read.

If I hadn't already heard the Flying Wedge single, I would have guessed Greg Corbin was a reggae musician. His photo exudes a cool, Rasta vibe. Matt and his brother have the same eyes and the same hair. Though Matt kept his short, it was still thick and practically untouched by gray despite his age (sixty-nine). He was also unusually tall and slim, with high cheekbones, almond eyes, and a regal bearing undiminished by his faded Detroit Tigers hat and slouchy jeans.

I ask Matt why he chose to surround himself with memento mori. "Because one day I'm going to die and I might see those people again," he says. "I want to remember that they're no longer here, but they may be somewhere else. Our culture makes you afraid to die, but there are a whole lotta cultures that existed before this one where they really weren't afraid to die. And sometimes people don't do some of the things they should do because they're afraid to die. And that even translates to 'Oh, I'll be embarrassed.' Because being embarrassed is kind of like dying." He pauses, then adds, "I've been embarrassed onstage, but it never stopped me."

Not everyone who comes to visit him likes the Room of Spirits, Matt confessed, but he enjoys gazing up at the funeral programs of his mother, grandparents, brother, uncles, friends, and a twelve-year-old boy from the neighborhood who was killed in a drive-by on New Year's Day a few years back.

"What's that old saying?" Matt laughs. "The dead can't hurt you. It's the living you've got to watch out for."

Ben Edmonds's theory about Flying Wedge was wrong. They were not isolated from the broader black rock community. They were neither outsider artists nor dilettantes. They were serious, heavy-gigging, committed musicians well known on the Detroit club circuit. Which isn't to say that Edmonds's impression of the music was off; it is safe to say that back in 1970, Flying Wedge was the heaviest, and strangest, rock band you'd never heard.

The Corbin brothers grew up solidly middle class in northwest Detroit and started playing music together when Greg was still in high school. While their parents weren't musical themselves (their father was a city bus driver, their mother worked in central booking at Detroit police headquarters), their father loved jazz enough to collect the autographs of Earl Father Hines, Ella Fitzgerald, Cab Calloway, and Count Basie, and to amass a prodigious collection of 78s. The boys were given music lessons while still in grade school: clarinet for Matt, who was intrigued by the instrument's strangeness and versatility, and guitar for Greg (who Matt suspects chose the instrument because of its resemblance to a woman's figure). They grew up on Motown and Stax—Martha Reeves was a neighbor and Diana Ross, a schoolmate—but after stumbling on the Isley Brothers' version of "Twist and Shout," specifically, a song called "The Spanish Twist" that featured Jimi Hendrix's electric guitar in place of a vocal line, they both began leaning in a harder, more experimental direction. Greg absorbed the influence of trailblazing guitarists like Charlie Byrd, who pushed the boundaries of Latin jazz, as well as classical players like Andres Segovia Torres and Joe Pass, while Matt got deep into Eddie Harris, a horn player whose free-ranging oeuvre spanned jazz, funk, R & B, and (disastrously) stand-up comedy.

Though the Corbin brothers played together informally while Greg was still in high school, the band only came together when Greg rejoined Matt in Detroit after earning a degree in biology at Tennessee State. The band's first incarnation was Penn Dixie, and it incorporated a cast of musicians equally esoteric in their tastes. Matt Corbin provided lead vocals and played an electric clarinet that sounded like something else entirely after he ran it through a maestro unit ("like a keyboard with toggle switches that allow you to get different kinds of sounds, a stereo sound, an oboe sound, a piccolo sound, a flute sound . . ."), an echoplex (which he manipulated to maximize feedback), and two piggy-back amps (to help "pump the sound out over the other instruments"). Their keyboardist was Elwin Rutledge, a guy Matt discovered tinkering around on the display piano at the local department store where they both worked. Rutledge played the Rock-Si-Chord, a proto-electric piano "invented in 1967 to approximate the sound of a harpsichord" (according to Wikipedia). Greg played a regular electric guitar, but he routinely ran it through three big amps when playing live, and layered it as many as ten times in the studio. Their childhood friend Vic Hill served as the band's drummer (he also doubled himself in the studio—the Flying Wedge single gives the impression of two different drummers playing concurrently), and their lineup included a rotating cast of bass players as well.

Soon they were getting gigs at colorful hotspots like Frantic Ernie Durham's Ballroom on Fenkell Street, the Roostertail, down by the waterfront, and the hippie hangouts lining Plum Street. They didn't know the guys in the band Death, but they knew a lot of big names in Detroit's black rock circuit.

"We knew Black Merda. We knew Little Charles. And we knew Tyrone Height," Matt told me. The music that had impressed Ben Blackwell as "created in a vacuum" was actually music created

alongside a lot of other legendary bands. Wedge's critic-seduc-
ing originality was actually the result of a very deliberate effort.
Black Merda—a pioneering experimental psych-rock quartet and
another brother-based band—were good friends from the neighborhood. Making sure they didn't cop Merda's style was a continual struggle, Matt confessed.

Locally, Flying Wedge was well known enough that they could
drop into clubs for impromptu sets, swapping instruments with
whomever was on the bill. Early on, the band's main problem
wasn't isolation, but the epic hassle of moving their own gear
around town. Penn Dixie couldn't achieve their signature sound
without at least six amps, and that's not counting the PA system
they often had to provide, or a drum kit. In order to reduce the
payload required just to rehearse, the band decided to move in
together. In 1967 they rented the house on Clairmount, which
was big enough to provide a bedroom for everyone. Before moving in together, they had rented a rehearsal space next to a doc-
tor's office but had to leave after being told the noise "disturbed
too many people." At the Clairmount house, they were far enough
from the neighbors that no one complained. But the freedom to
finally turn up their amps as loud as they wanted created a new
problem.

"There would be times when our amplifiers would catch on
fire, we would be playing that loud," Matt chuckled. "And it
would take us two weeks before we could get new speakers."
Money was always an issue; Matt still remembers it cost $60 to
replace an amp. "We'd say, 'Well, we'll just be quiet for a while,
put our money together and get another speaker.'"

Though Penn Dixie never released a record, they did make a
number of recordings at Artie Field's studio, a local "jingle house"
within walking distance of the house on Clairmount. Occasion-
ally Elwin pulled strings to get them into United Sound, the legendary studio where Barry Gordy produced his first Motown

record in 1959. But without money or label backing, this meant resorting to minor subterfuge.

"We'd have to wait around for other guys to do whatever they were doing and then we'd get a chance to do something. It wasn't like we had carte blanche in these places. We used to sneak into places to do stuff."

Matt doesn't remember how many of these sessions took place. What is known is that nothing ever happened with these recordings. They had enough material for a record, Matt explained, but Penn Dixie just "never had the management that could take us to the level of saying, 'Well, you're gonna actually put this record out.'"

It wasn't for lack of trying—an impressive roster of Motor City power brokers cycled through the house on Clairmount to hear the band play, including famed Motown producer Harvey Fuqua.

"He thought we were crazy." Matt laughed. "We weren't what Motown was looking for. We were making hard rock. See, we were punk before it was punk, but we were not as blatant as punk is. In other words, we weren't trying to go out and have a side of ourselves that was offensive to some people. But we were trying to be expressive in a way where we're going to say what we *want* to say." Nor, Matt contended, were they a good fit for radio airplay. "There were the soul stations and then there was the 101, WRIF. We were in between both of them."

Eventually, Elwin (who would go on to become a successful producer in LA, writing music for artists like Grammy Award–winning singer Jennifer Hudson) secured a sponsor for the band. The only thing the band knew about the guy was that his name was Bernie, he was a producer, and he had a lot money. But when they looked at the contract Bernie handed them, they interpreted the deal as, "I'm gonna put money in you guys, but then you guys belong to me." Flying Wedge had watched too many talented musicians sign disastrous contracts—no one was even tempted.

But with the fade-out of the mysterious "Bernie," so went the band's last chance at broader recognition. When the owner of the house on Clairmount finally announced he was selling, it forced the band's hand. Only Matt and Greg (who had jobs working for the city, as a public school art teacher and a city building inspector, respectively) had the means to buy the house, and even that meant pawning most of the band's equipment. After five years together, the band's split was undramatic. (It's hard to imagine any split from Matt Corbin as being dramatic—during our time together on his front porch, there wasn't a passerby who didn't stop to greet him by name, and his two phones rarely stopped ringing.) The remainder of Penn Dixie found new bands. Matt Corbin got married in 1972; his first daughter was born soon after. He started putting more energy into his art career, and teaching. His brother, meanwhile, retired to the other half of the house, which was divided into a duplex. He took the entire Penn Dixie archive with him. Greg Corbin called his new solo project Flying Wedge, but it was built on the pyre of Penn Dixie's old songs—the only difference being that now Greg alone had full creative control.

His brother was always rehearsing, eventually becoming dexterous enough with his tone that he could make the guitar "sound just about any way he wanted." Sometimes Greg would ask Matt to write some lyrics for whatever song he was tracking, or to lay down some lead vocals, and Matt, hearing the isolated tracks, would swear he was listening to an organ or some other instrument. But usually it was just his brother, playing guitar.

Given their unusual closeness, physical proximity, and continued collaboration, it's strange that Matt Corbin doesn't really know how the Flying Wedge single was recorded. (He couldn't even recall whether his brother owned a flying wedge, Gibson's Flying V guitar, which inspired the name of the band.) Sometimes Matt claimed that his brother had played all of the instruments on

"I Can't Believe" and "Come to My Casbah" himself. Other times he said Vic Hill and/or other former members of Penn Dixie might have played on the single. Sometimes he claimed the songs were recorded in a studio, other times that part (or all) of the songs were tracked by Greg, possibly right there at the house on Clairmount. Matt also had no knowledge of his brother's visit to the *CREEM* offices or of who accompanied him. But he told me he's sure his brother had no idea that the editor of *CREEM* magazine was looking for him. Or that WABX had ever spun the Flying Wedge single.

Matt could only hint at his brother's musical frustrations sideways, in the third person: "A guitarist can't always do the kind of solo that they feel inside of themselves in a record that's going to be played on the radio." Or: "We learned from people who kept dropping bombs that sooner or later you're going to hit the target." Or: "Greg was the kind of guy who didn't have a lot to say if there was a question he didn't want to answer." I came away from my conversation with Matt with a lot of superficial knowledge of Greg Corbin: that he started college wanting to be a dentist until the lure of music became too strong, that he earned so much overtime from the Detroit city government that his name was included in a newspaper article about the excesses of municipal spending, and that he sank the majority of that money into music. I know that it was Greg's incessant playing and continual impulse to gather eclectic musicians around him that inspired his brother to seriously pursue music as a career, not vice versa. And I know that Greg was willing to tolerate a lot if it meant achieving a better sound, going so far as to recruit a bassist from a local halfway house, Matt told me, because he was so enthralled by the guy's plucking technique. But no matter how many questions I asked, I never got any sense of Greg Corbin's emotional core, or his driving aesthetic philosophy. Maybe the many eerie parallels with the other Detroit proto-punk, brother-based band, Death, have conditioned me to expect these answers. Of the three Hackney brothers who comprised Death, it was also their guitarist, David, who was the visionary of the group. And like Greg Corbin, David died young of cancer (at age forty-eight, only one year after Corbin succumbed in 2000 at the age of fifty-two). Both Death and Flying Wedge only released five hundred copies of a solitary single—Death in 1976, Flying Wedge in 1972—that failed to sell. But unlike Greg Corbin, David Hackney had always been extremely clear, adamant even, about what drove him and what Death was about, from the band's name (which didn't exactly endear them to audiences in the feel-good era of disco) to its powerful iconography. He even left behind a prophesy when he put the band's master tapes into the hands of his brother, Bobby Hackney, shortly before he died, telling him, "Bob, you've got to keep all this stuff. The world's going to come looking for it one day. And when the world comes looking for it, I'll know that you'll have it."

Greg Corbin didn't hand any prophesies to his brother, but he left behind a lot of tapes. Soon after Penn Dixie broke up and the Flying Wedge single floundered, a vertical TEAC reel-to-reel recorder became the sole repository of his musical output for the next twenty-five years.

"My brother was never married. He had so many girlfriends that would come by here and throw rocks at his window to get him to open the door," Matt says. "Even to this day—and my brother's been gone since 1999—there are still girls today, when they see me they say, 'Where is your brother? I'm looking for him.' And because I don't want to go into a long explanation of what happened, I just tell them, 'He's out of town.'"

It was when one of his brother's women called the house and asked Matt what his brother was doing in the hospital that Matt first learned Greg had cancer. Initially Matt scoffed at the idea, thinking this was just Greg trying to put another girl off his scent. But his brother wasn't answering his door, and no one at work knew where he was. A call to the hospital confirmed that what the woman said was true. When Matt arrived, his brother was blunt. "I had cancer," he said. "They cut it out." It was his liver. "I'm gonna be OK," Greg added. "Don't tell nobody."

Though shocked that Greg had kept his cancer a secret, Matt reluctantly agreed. "I lived with my brother all my life, so I'm going do what he says. I didn't tell anybody."

Eventually the cancer went into remission and Greg resumed working. But months later, it returned. There was another operation and more rounds of chemo, during which Matt continued to keep Greg's deteriorating health a secret from their parents and sister (all of whom remained in Detroit), as well as their many mutual friends. But when Greg finally admitted there was nothing more the doctors could do, Matt convinced his brother to come clean. Soon afterward, Greg moved in with their mother, who nursed him until the end of his life.

Driving down Clairmount today, you get the Bladerunner version of Detroit. Gaping mouths of ruined houses. City blocks eerily gone to prairie. Abandoned cars puddled on flat tires. It's a visual allegory of Detroit's decline after the 1967 race riots, which began on the corner of Twelfth and Clairmount. When the Corbins moved in with their Penn Dixie bandmates, the neighborhood, though on the downward slope, was still humming. There was a General Motors plant nearby on Second Avenue, and the city bus still made frequent stops on Clairmount. Today the apartment buildings that used to face the house are gone, replaced by an empty lot where Matt Corbin's *Geome Tree* installation still stands. Traffic is nonexistent.

The house itself is an oasis on an otherwise grim block. It is surrounded by Matt's latest sculptures, a collection of free-standing monochromatic collages of salvaged junk that explode from the ground like apocalyptic sunflowers. The front of the house, which Matt rebuilt himself, is cocooned in a massive greenhouse that extends over the front porch and what used to be a garage. Hundreds of plants clamor against the sharply angled panes. Stepping inside, I felt as though I'd left the city for some strange subtropical zone. Yet it too was built from the debris of scrapped houses and factories, by Matt himself.

It feels somehow fitting that a book that began with Madonna should end here, at a house that once belonged to a band with three fans.

Greg's archive remains in his half of the house, untouched since he died fifteen years ago. It includes the Penn Dixie material, boxes of the vanishingly rare Flying Wedge single and the less rare but still sought-after "Miraculous" 7-inch, Greg's TEAC machine, and the solo tapes he kept making up until cancer left him bedridden. But it also contains Greg's artwork, his notebooks, footage from an abandoned music video shot on Beta for a song called "Fast Delivery" that was ambitious enough, according to Matt, to require the purchase of a junked car. What's all this worth? Maybe nothing. But the music industry is officially interested. Two weeks before I arrived in Detroit, Ben Blackwell came to visit Matt. They spent two hours together, during which Ben asked to review Greg Corbin's archive on behalf of Third Man Records. Rob Severin from Numero Records had also been courting Corbin, recently sending him a care package filled with vinyl.

Matt claims to be excited about the surge of interest in his brother's music and the possibility of a mainstream release. But the more I talk to him, the more I realize he is excited about everything: his art, his grandkids, his plants, his ever-expanding house, his neighborhood. He is the youngest-seeming, happiest, most forward-thinking almost-seventy-year-old I have ever met. (Maybe we should all start decorating our living rooms with funeral programs?) Matt's even talking about putting Penn Dixie back together, and recently got in touch with Vic Hill and Elwin again. But every time I ask why he hasn't gone through his brother's tapes, he offers a different excuse. He worries the TEAC player might be broken ("Greg was the one who could always fix that stuff") or that plunging into the archive would throw his own musical and artistic projects off track. And I feel like offering a gentle prompt: "Or maybe it's just really hard to go through your dead brother's stuff?" But if Matt isn't shaken after spending twenty minutes describing his brother's death from liver cancer, it's not my business to make him so.

Knowing so much about Flying Wedge, but having heard so little of the music, there is a selfish part of me that finds Matt Corbin's inertia maddening. I want to wait until he goes inside, run around to the Greg side of the house, and pry the back door open. But another part, I have to admit, is relieved. In an age when George Clinton is offering to call up fans and record their outgoing voicemail message for $250, and we swim daily in the flotsam of pop stars' wrecked lives, rock 'n' roll still retains some of its mysteries. Or maybe there is no mystery. Maybe, as Matt told me, Greg just "thought playing guitar was the coolest thing you could do. And that's what he wanted to do. And that's what he did." For some people rock 'n' roll is about fame; for others it's all about the quest to make real the music they hear in their head. Greg Corbin did that.

Seven months after my trip to Detroit, I emailed Ben Blackwell: did the Flying Wedge archive live up to expectation? Blackwell had no idea.

Matt Corbin still hadn't opened the door.

To be honest, attempting to write a book about Madonna nearly drove me insane.

Every day that I woke up to write about one woman's massive musical success was also a day that I was forced to confront my own failure. Just as I was trying to chart the meteoric rise of Madonna's career, the last of the four labels that put out my albums quietly folded. I had been holding out hope for one day making another record—you know, roaring back onto the indie scene with another hooky collection of songs about existential despair—yet it had become clear that survival required embracing a particularly Madonnalike mode of aggressive self-promotion. This was depressing not just because of what it boded for my return to music, but because all of my favorite artists—perhaps the most well-loved, genre-shattering artists of any era—tended to be weird, difficult, non-Madonnalike people. It was hard to imagine the chronically depressed folk troubadour Nick Drake putting stickers advertising his website on bathroom walls, or urging fans to "upvote" his demo submission to Muzooka.com so that he could play a showcase at Webster Hall.

I had spent the majority of my twenties and a good half of my thirties doing whatever I could to lever myself up the indie rock ladder, only to discover that the terminal point I'd be hurtling myself toward was actually zooming away at twice the rate. Indie labels were dying. A&R budgets were shriveling. Many of the artists I'd spent my teenaged years admiring were going back to bartending, or teaching guitar. Had I been born ten years later and grown up a child of Napster and Myspace, I might have watched these nineties relics die dry-eyed, but I grew up at a time when it was actually possible to eke out a living making niche-music. Fans of grunge were hungry for songs just as strange and unrepentant as Nirvana's had seemed when they punched through the iron curtain of '80s corporate rock, and labels responded to that demand by shining their klieg lights on genres like slo-core and emo and riot grrl, heretofore the exclusive provinces of geeky college radio DJs, record shop clerks, and fan-zine readers.

I absorbed all these influences and drank in all this hope just as music piracy began making itself felt on the street. Between 2003 and 2008 alone, more than 3,100 record stores in America closed, 80 of them in the city where I lived (New York). Record labels, music magazines, recording studios were suddenly being eulogized everywhere. Music had turned into an idea, into conversation, into nature, into air. It was infinite and free and, paradoxically, only getting better and weirder and more innovative with every passing year. Unlike eating endangered salmon for dinner every night, gorging oneself at the all-you-can-listen-to music buffet didn't seem to have any tangible impact on either the quality or quantity of music being produced. While there was no downside for consumers, for those indie-rockers who actually made an income from album sales, and the grassroots labels that supported them, there was a growing sense of panic. But panicking about money and the future and quotidian things like health insurance and food was the antithesis of indie cool—and "cool" was still the currency of the rock world. Very few musicians were willing to admit the real financial impact file-sharing had on their incomes. So most stuck to mild pronouncements, exhorting fans to "support independent music." To be honest about their increasing struggle to pay rent would be to open themselves to the same dark criticisms that clawed their own hearts at night—that the problem wasn't piracy, it was *them*. Their music just wasn't good enough. Or they were too old. Or their fans had moved on. That it was their fault, essentially, and they were just bitter. Every article about the "death of the music industry" trailed long, venomous tentacles of comments in this vein from the let-music-be-free crowd, telling musicians the onus was on them: they needed to innovate, work their social networks, Catch the Wave, Think Different, Just Do It.

In large part, the digital revolution didn't snuff out the music industry by unshackling songs from any conceivable artifact that took up retail space; it killed it by revealing musicians as the false prophets of commerce we'd been all along. The bald truth is that musicians will keep making music regardless of whether we get paid or not. Because we love it. Because we have to. Because every other job we ever had felt fake and wrong and painful. Because to fall in love with music—with art of any kind—is to lock yourself into the cab of a speeding truck with shot brakes; it's the kind of affair that ends only when you hit the guardrail.

But Madonna isn't just a musician; she is the "whole package" and a *real* prophet of commerce. Which is why it is wrong, and kind of stupid, to compare her to Flying Wedge or Sinead O'Connor or especially to me.

She is also an artist. One might even call her an artist of commerce; someone with the rare talent to know exactly what the public craves without knowing they crave it.

The thing Madonna intuited almost immediately when she reached New York, a city awash with the human flotsam of shipwrecked ambition, was that succeeding as an artist meant mastering two entirely different trades. There was the honing-your-craft part (a pleasurable compulsion for most), and then there was *the hustle*, that ego-eroding whetstone against which much creative promise is dashed.

Madonna's whole-hearted, unapologetic embrace of the hustle is what distinguished her from her peers. She was, from the onset, a sort of hybrid mythological beast: the body of a dancer, the voice of a temptress, and the mind of a businesswoman. Qualities that earned her respect and revulsion in equal measure. From the start she pursued her ambition on parallel tracks, even as she struggled to form a C chord on boyfriend/bandmate Dan Gilroy's guitar.

"She'd be up in the morning, a quick cup of coffee, then right to the phones, calling up everybody—everybody," Gilroy told *Rolling Stone* in 1984. "Everyone from Bleecker Bob's [a famous Village record shop] to potential management. Anything and everything. . . . I knew that with that kind of drive and devotion to getting ahead something had to happen."

And Madonna has never been anything but aggressively honest about her ambition. When Dick Clark interviewed her on American Bandstand in 1984 (an interview that began with Madonna explaining she was born in Detroit), Clark asked about the period in her life when she broke off from all the doggy-paddling bands she'd been performing with to try making it on her own.

"Were you the least bit scared?" Clark asked.

"Not really," Madonna smiled. "I think I've always had a lot of confidence in myself."

"We are a couple of weeks from the New Year," Clark continued. "What do you hope will happen, not only in 1984 but for the rest of your professional life? What are your dreams?"

"Um . . ." Madonna says, her face exploding into a can-you-believe-I'm-actually-saying-this grin. "To rule the world!"

This was the same exact answer she gave the Sire Records A&R rep Michael Rosenblatt, the person responsible for getting

Madonna her first record contract. "She came by on that Monday and played me that demo," Rosenblatt told *Rolling Stone* in 2013. "It wasn't amazing. But this girl sitting in my office was just radiating star power. I asked her, 'What are you looking for in this?' I always ask that, and the wrong answer is, 'I want to get my art out,' because this is a business. And Madonna's answer was, 'I want to rule the world.'"

If she had only wanted to rule Bay City, or even certain neighborhoods of New York, she wouldn't have had a career. But she wanted to rule the world, and went on to do just that. I suspect that more than any qualms we may have about Madonna's music or nip-slips, or her treatment of religious icons or choice of men, her bombastic and self-prophetic confidence is what most accounts for the animus against her. In 1985, while hypothesizing as to the karmic source of her enormous popularity, Madonna told *Time* magazine, "Maybe my fearlessness and courage give people a good feeling." But maybe her fearlessness and courage, in equal measure, give people a bad feeling, prompting an enraged and desperate little internal voice to sputter, *What makes you think you are so much better than anyone else? That you have the right to claim all of these impossibly grand things you seek? You are just a middle-class girl from Michigan so you better start acting like it!*

I wonder if perhaps we aren't talking to ourselves when we ask these questions. And whether our criticism is really a veiled reproach in the face of what Madonna has so defiantly proven is possible. *Why didn't you think you were good enough? Why didn't you dream bigger? What made you think you didn't have the right to grander things? And why didn't you try harder to get them?*

Maybe these are the questions we are really asking ourselves when we confront our dislike of Madonna.

And maybe by "we," I mean me.

Almost exactly one year after Commissioner Chris Girard's signage resolution was approved, Gary Johnson sent me the following email.

Subject line: No Happy Endings.

Hi Alina:

I hope all is well with you and your family. We've been back in Essexville for three or four weeks now. My Madonna class is going well at SVSU [Saginaw Valley State University], but I had the fewest sign-ups (28) for any of the many classes that I've offered there.

I interviewed Chris Girard before we left for the Christmas holidays in NJ. He had nothing to report concerning the possibility of the Madonna sign going up at the Bradley House (the former site of Mercy Hospital). It's been two months since that interview; and I have not heard anything else about the sign, the development of a fund to collect money for the sign, or the international contest that was supposed to be set up for design ideas for the Madonna sign.

Although Girard was coy about the possibility of his running for mayor when I spoke with him, he did announce his candidacy a week or so ago. What this means for the continuation of Madonna-related projects remains to be seen.

As I read Gary's message, I marveled again at how this totally abstract thing, the notion that Madonna *was here*, had managed to generate so much discussion and hand-wringing, so much introspection, so many plans, so much activity, so much failure, and so much hope, in so many different spheres. It was almost as though she were no longer a person, but a talisman: magical contagion incarnate. And I could imagine a day in the distant future, millenia from now when humankind has evolved beyond music and videos and celebrity-branded perfumes, when Madonna will decouple from her flesh-based accomplishments entirely to become pure abstraction. Morphing from a noun into an adjective or verb, one that summons a restless dissatisfaction with the status quo or arouses the threat of a boundaryless freedom.

Or maybe all that will remain of Madonna is a conceptual understanding of some very specific centrifugal point in the human psyche, one that may differ depending on whom you ask, but that every person must ultimately define themselves as being either for or against.

If I had to guess, that would probably be just fine with her.

June 4, 2015

THANKS

To Gary Johnson for leading me on this journey—a journey that perhaps ended up being a circle, but was highly enjoyable nonetheless—and to the many people I interviewed for this book, who showed me their tattoos, read my Madonna horoscope, and provided tours of their funereally themed living rooms.

To the two Bens, Ben Edmonds and Ben Blackwell, for sharing the story of Flying Wedge.

To Dan Engber, for emergency journalistic counsel and for inspiring by example. You have an unerring sense for where the story lies. Or, as often happens in our case, the nonstory. Anyway, I'm lucky to have you on speed-dial.

To Casey Kittrell and David Menconi, who launched this madcap adventure, and to my book agent, Anna Stein, for providing clear-eyed editorial advice at the moment it was most needed.

To Jason Mellard, whose blueprint for revising this book ended up being my salvation. You are a very fine writer yourself, and I look forward to reading your books.

To Sue Carter, whom I hope has recovered from my bad grammar by now, and to Lynne Chapman, who made sure this book didn't fly off the rails just when the train was finally entering the station.

To Amanda Palmer, for moral support and crucial Madonna insight. (No backsies, no givesies, no regretsies—not a bad life motto, really.)

To my parents, who suggested I should be a writer back in elementary school, then patiently waited a few decades while things shook themselves out.

To Eric Chinski. As long as I keep writing, I'm just going to have to keep thanking you.

And to Joshua and Zoe: without you, life would just be a sad cup of decaf coffee.